The Management Task

Titles in the Institute of Management Series

NVQ level 3
The Competent First-Line Manager
Shields

Certificate (NVQ level 4)
The Management Task (second edition)
Dixon

Managing Financial Resources (second edition)
Broadbent and Cullen

Managing Information (second edition)
Wilson

Managing People (second edition)
Thomson

Meeting Customer Needs (second edition)
Smith

Personal Effectiveness (second edition)
Murdock and Scutt

Diploma (NVQ level 5)
Developing Human Resources
Thomson and Mabey

Managerial Finance
Parkinson

Managing an Effective Operation
Fowler and Graves

Managing Knowledge
Wilson

Managing in the Public Sector
Blundell and Murdock

Managing Quality
Wilson, McBride and Bell

Managing Schools
Whitaker

Managing in the Single European Market
Brown

Marketing
Lancaster and Reynolds

Tutor Support
NVQ Handbook: practical guidelines
for providers and assessors
Walton

The Management Task

Second edition

Rob Dixon

Published in association with
the Institute of Management

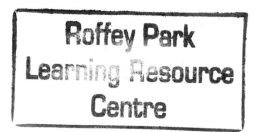

the Institute
of Management

BUTTERWORTH
HEINEMANN

Butterworth-Heinemann
Linacre House, Jordan Hill, Oxford OX2 8DP
225 Wildwood Avenue, Woburn, MA 01801-2041
A division of Reed Educational and Professional Publishing Ltd

Ⓡ A member of the Reed Elsevier plc group

OXFORD   AUCKLAND   BOSTON
JOHANNESBURG   MELBOURNE   NEW DELHI

First published 1993
Reprinted 1993 (twice), 1994
Second edition 1997
Reprinted 1998, 1999, 2000, 2001, 2002

British Library Cataloguing in Publication Data
A catalogue record for this book is available from the British Library

ISBN 0 7506 3390 5

For more information on all Butterworth-Heinemann
publications please visit our website at www.bh.com

Typeset by Avocet Typesetting, Brill, Aylesbury, Bucks
Printed and bound in Great Britain by Biddles Ltd
www.biddles.co.uk

FOR EVERY TITLE THAT WE PUBLISH, BUTTERWORTH-HEINEMANN
WILL PAY FOR BTCV TO PLANT AND CARE FOR A TREE.

Contents

Series adviser's preface

This book is one of a series designed for people wanting to develop their capabilities as managers. You might think that there isn't anything very new in that. In one way you would be right. The fact that very many people want to learn to become better managers is not new, and for many years a wide range of approaches to such learning and development has been available. These have included courses leading to formal qualifications, organizationally-based management development programmes and a whole variety of self-study materials. A copious literature, extending from academic textbooks to sometimes idiosyncratic prescriptions from successful managers and consultants, has existed to aid – or perhaps confuse – the potential seeker after managerial truth and enlightenment.

So what is new about this series? In fact, a great deal – marking in some ways a revolution in our thinking both about the art of managing and also the process of developing managers.

Where did it all begin? Like most revolutions, although there may be a single, identifiable act that precipitated the uprising, the roots of discontent are many and long-established. The debate about the performance of British managers, the way managers are educated and trained, and the extent to which shortcomings in both these areas have contributed to our economic decline, has been running for several decades.

Until recently, this debate had been marked by periods of frenetic activity – stimulated by some report or enquiry and perhaps ending in some new initiatives or policy changes – followed by relatively long periods of comparative calm. But the underlying causes for concern persisted. Basically, the majority of managers in the UK appeared to have little or no training for their role, certainly far less than their counterparts in our major competitor nations. And there was concern about the nature, style and appropriateness of the management education and training that was available.

The catalyst for this latest revolution came in late 1986 and early 1987, when three major reports reopened the whole issue. The 1987 reports were *The Making of British Managers* by John Constable and Robert McCormick, carried out for the British Institute of Management and the CBI, and *The Making of Managers* by Charles Handy, carried out for the (then) Manpower Services Commission, National Economic Development Office and British Institute of Management. The 1986 report, which often receives less recognition than it deserves as a key contribution to the recent changes, was *Management Training: context and process* by Iain Mangham and Mick Silver, carried out for the Economic and Social Research Council and the Department of Trade and Industry.

It is not the place to review in detail what the reports said. Indeed, they and their consequences are discussed in several places in this series of books. But essentially they confirmed that:

- British managers were undertrained by comparison with their counterparts internationally.
- The majority of employers invested far too little in training and developing their managers.
- Many employers found it difficult to specify with any degree of detail just what it was that they required successful managers to be able to do.

The Constable/McCormick and Handy reports advanced various recommendations for addressing these problems, involving an expansion of management education and development, a reformed structure of qualifications and a commitment from employers to a code of practice for management development. While this analysis was not new, and had echoes of much that had been said in earlier debates, this time a few leading individuals determined that the response should be both radical and permanent. The response was coordinated by the newly-established Council for Management Education and Development (now the National Forum for Management Education and Development (NFMED)) under the energetic and visionary leadership of Bob (now Sir Bob) Reid, formerly of Shell UK and the British Railways Board.

Under the umbrella of NFMED a series of employer-led working parties tackled the problem of defining what it was that managers should be able to do, and how this differed for people at different levels in their organizations; how this satisfactory ability to perform might be verified; and how an appropriate structure of management qualifications could be put in place. This work drew upon the methods used to specify vocational standards in industry and commerce, and led to the development and introduction of competence-based management standards and qualifications. In this context, competence is defined as the ability to perform the activities within an occupation or function to the standards expected in employment.

It is this competence-based approach that is new in our thinking about the manager's capabilities. It is also what is new about this series of books, in that they are designed to support both this new structure of management standards, and of development activities based on it. The series was originally commissioned to support the Institute of Management's Certificate and Diploma qualifications, which were one of the first to be based on the new standards. However, these books are equally appropriate to any university, college or indeed company course leading to a certificate in management or diploma in management studies.

The standards were specified through an extensive process of consultation with a large number of managers in organizations of many different types and sizes. They are therefore employment-based and employer-supported. And they fill the gap that Mangham and Silver identified – now we do have a language to describe what it is employers want their managers to be able to do – at least in part.

If you are engaged in any form of management development leading to a certificate or diploma qualification conforming to the national management standards, then you are probably already familiar with most of the key ideas on which the standards are based. To achieve their key purpose, which is defined as achieving the organization's objectives and continuously improving its performance, managers need to perform four key roles: managing operations, managing finance, managing people and managing information. Each of these key roles has a sub-structure of units and elements, each with associated performance and assessment criteria.

The reason for the qualification 'in part' is that organizations are different, and jobs within them are different. Thus the generic management standards probably do not cover all the management competences that you may need to possess in your job. There are almost certainly additional things, specific to your own situation in your own organization, that you need to be able to do. The standards are necessary, but almost certainly not sufficient. Only you, in discussion with your boss, will be able to decide what other capabilities you need to possess. But the standards are a place to start, a basis on which to build. Once you have demonstrated your proficiency against the standards, it will stand you in good stead as you progress through your organization, or change jobs.

So how do the new standards change the process by which you develop yourself as a manager? They change the process of development, or of gaining a management qualification, quite a lot. It is no longer a question of acquiring information and facts, perhaps by being 'taught' in some classroom environment, and then being tested to see what you can recall. It involves demonstrating, in a quite specific way, that you can do certain things to a particular standard of performance. And because of this, it puts a much greater onus on you to manage your own development, to decide how you can demonstrate any particular competence, what evidence you need to present, and how you can collect it. Of course, there will always be people to advise and guide you in this, if you need help.

But there is another dimension, and it is to this that this series of books is addressed. While the standards stress ability to perform, they do not ignore the traditional knowledge base that has been associated with 'management studies'. Rather, they set this in a different context. The standards are supported by 'underpinning knowledge and understanding' which has three components:

- Purpose and context, which is knowledge and understanding of the manager's objectives, and of the relevant organizational and environmental influences, opportunities and values.
- Principles and methods, which is knowledge and understanding of the theories, models, principles, methods and

techniques that provide the basis of competent managerial performance.
- Data, which is knowledge and understanding of specific facts likely to be important to meeting the standards.

Possession of the relevant knowledge and understanding underpinning the standards is needed to support competent managerial performance as specified in the standards. It also has an important role in supporting the transferability of management capabilities. It helps to ensure that you have done more than learned 'the way we do things around here' in your own organization. It indicates a recognition of the wider things which underpin competence, and that you will be able to change jobs or organizations and still be able to perform effectively.

These books cover the knowledge and understanding underpinning the management standards, most specifically in the category of principles and methods. But their coverage is not limited to the minimum required by the standards, and extends in both depth and breadth in many areas. The authors have tried to approach these underlying principles and methods in a practical way. They use many short cases and examples which we hope will demonstrate how, in practice, the principles and methods, and knowledge of purpose and context plus data, support the ability to perform as required by the management standards. In particular we hope that this type of presentation will enable you to identify and learn from similar examples in your own managerial work.

You will already have noticed that one consequence of this new focus on the standards is that the traditional 'functional' packages of knowledge and theory do not appear. The standard textbook titles such as 'quantitative methods', 'production management', 'organizational behaviour', etc. disappear. Instead, principles and methods have been collected together in clusters that more closely match the key roles within the standards. You will also find a small degree of overlap in some of the volumes, because some principles and methods support several of the individual units within the standards. We hope you will find this reinforcement useful.

Having described the positive aspects of standards-based management development, it would be wrong to finish without a few cautionary remarks. The developments described above may seem simple, logical and uncontroversial. It did not always seem that way in the years of work which led up to the introduction of the standards. To revert to the revolution analogy, the process has been marked by ideological conflict and battles over sovereignty and territory. It has sometimes been unclear which side various parties are on – and indeed how many sides there are! The revolution, if well advanced, is not at an end. Guerrilla warfare continues in parts of the territory.

Perhaps the best way of describing this is to say that, while competence-based standards are widely recognized as at least a major part of the answer to improving managerial performance, they are not the whole answer. There is still some debate about the way competences are defined, and whether those in the standards are the most appropriate on which to base assessment of managerial performance. There are other models of management competences than those in the standards.

There is also a danger in separating management performance into a set of discrete components. The whole is, and needs to be, more than the sum of the parts. Just like bowling an off-break in cricket, practising a golf swing or forehand drive in tennis, you have to combine all the separate movements into a smooth, flowing action. How you combine the competences, and build on them, will mark your own individual style as a manager.

We should also be careful not to see the standards as set in stone. They determine what today's managers need to be able to do. As the arena in which managers operate changes, then so will the standards. The lesson for all of us as managers is that we need to go on learning and developing, acquiring new skills or refining existing ones. Obtaining your certificate or diploma is like passing a mile post, not crossing the finishing line.

All the changes and developments of recent years have brought management qualifications, and the processes by which they are gained, much closer to your job as a manager. We hope these books support this process by providing bridges between your own experience and the underlying principles and methods which will help you to demonstrate your competence. Already, there is a lot of evidence that managers enjoy the challenge of demonstrating competence, and find immediate benefits in their jobs from the programmes based on these new-style qualifications. We hope you do too. Good luck in your career development.

Paul Jervis

Preface

This book was written as part of an exciting cooperative venture between Butterworth-Heinemann and the Institute of Management to provide accessible material on management, its processes and functions.

This book considers both the nature of management and the environment in which management operates. The requirements for effective, successful management techniques are explored; covering many areas from the need for planning and forecasting, leadership, motivation and communication, to control, decision-making and the management of personnel.

I would like to extend my gratitude to all those who have helped in the production of this book, particularly to Charlotte Ridings for her background research and to my wife Ann for her patience.

Rob Dixon

Part One
Introduction

1 Introduction

WHAT IS 'THE MANAGEMENT TASK'?

The task of management is all about organizing groups of people to work together productively towards known, clear goals, or objectives. There are many different levels of management, from production foremen, hospital ward sisters and senior secretaries, all supervising small groups of employees, to managing directors and chief executives, responsible for directing large multinational companies and organizations. However, the basic description of the management task holds good for all managers, regardless of their seniority.

Unfortunately, management is not quite as simple as that! The manager's job is very wide ranging. Mintzberg (1973) analysed the roles managers have to adopt during their work and listed seven major ones, as follows:

1 The entrepreneur: the manager as planner and risk-taker.
2 The resource allocator: the manager as organizer and coordinator.
3 The figurehead/leader: the manager as motivator and coordinator.
4 The liaisor/disseminator: the manager as coordinator and communicator.
5 The monitor: the manager as controller.
6 The spokesperson/negotiator: the manager as motivator and communicator.
7 The disturbance-handler: the manager as motivator and coordinator.

Thus we can see that the manager's job is to plan, take decisions, motivate, lead and organize the employees that he/she is responsible for, communicate with them and control and coordinate their work. In Part Two these management processes of planning, motivating, etc., will each be looked at in detail.

WHY MANAGEMENT IS IMPORTANT

Good management is vital if a business or any other enterprise is to be successful. Drucker (1967) regards an effective management team as the one big advantage a company can have over its competitors:

> In a competitive economy, above all, the quality and performance of the managers determine the success of a business, indeed they determine its survival. For the quality and performance of its managers is the only effective advantage an enterprise in a competitive economy can have.

Effective management can transform an inefficient, underperforming organization into a profitable, sound business, but the reverse is also true. Ineffectual managers can ruin sound businesses by allowing them to stagnate, content to rely on past achievements rather than looking for new challenges. No doubt you can think of examples of both kinds of management in companies or just departments that you are familiar with.

THE DEVELOPMENT OF MODERN MANAGEMENT IDEAS

Before we go on to look at the processes involved in the management task, the rest of this chapter will give a little background information about the changes in management thinking over the years, which should give you an insight into how and why organizations are run in the ways they are today.

It should be remembered that, naturally, each theory reflects the thinking and attitudes of its time. But it is clear that they still have a lot of influence on today's business methods and ideas.

Theories about the best way to manage people have developed over the years from the beginning of the century. The three main schools of thought are the classical school, the human relations school, and the systems school of management. Figure 1.1 shows how the different theories have developed over time, and have built upon previous ideas.

The classical school

The classical approach to management concentrated on trying to form general principles of management. These principles, it was hoped, could then be applied to all organizations in every business situation. Techniques of mass-production were just beginning to be widely used, and managers were concerned to find the most economical method of producing the greatest number of goods.

The solution of the classical theorists was to divide work tasks up into their constituent parts. Thus, for example, instead of a cobbler making one complete pair of shoes, from the initial cutting of the leather right through to the final buffing and polishing of the finished article, before starting afresh on a different pair, the jobs would be divided between several workers. One would cut the leather for all the shoes to be made that day, another would stretch the leather, and so on.

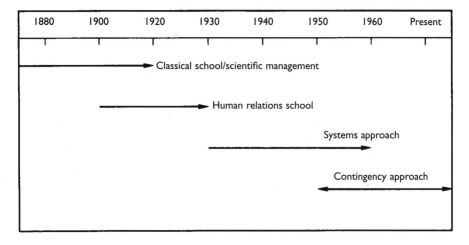

Figure 1.1 Developments in management theory

The main writers of the classical school were F. W. Taylor, Henri Fayol, Frank and Lillian Gilbreth, and Henry Gantt.

F. W. TAYLOR AND SCIENTIFIC MANAGEMENT

Taylor (1856–1915), whose ideas were developed when he was a manager at a steel works in the USA, was concerned with the formal structure and activities of organizations, i.e. the optimum numbers of employees that each manager should supervise, work division, etc. Taylor believed in, and pioneered the use of, scientific methods of observation and analysis in management.

THE PRINCIPLES BEHIND SCIENTIFIC MANAGEMENT

In *Principles of Scientific Management* (1911) Taylor set out the fundamental principles which he thought underlay scientific management. These can be summed up as follows:

> 1 Replacing rules of thumb with a true science of work. Many
>   companies relied (and some still do!) upon information

retained in the heads of employees, rather than gathering all that knowledge together and making a proper record of it. Taylor felt that without this reliance upon the 'it has always been done this way' mentality, 'every single subject, large and small, becomes the question for scientific investigation, for reduction to law' (Taylor, 1911).

2 Replacing 'chaotic individualism' with cooperation between managers and employees to the mutual benefit of all.

3 The scientific selection and progressive development of workers, i.e. workers should be given jobs which they are best suited to do, and carefully trained to do these jobs. This would be to the advantage of both companies and employees, allowing both groups to prosper.

4 Working for maximum output rather than restricted output.

Taylor's aim in his system of scientific management was to increase the efficiency of production methods, not just to lower company costs and thus increase profits, but also to enable the workers to increase their productivity and so earn higher wages. Through scientific methods of job analysis, establishing the best, most efficient way of doing the work, and through training the workers in these efficient production methods, greater productivity could, Taylor believed, be achieved. Scientific management would eliminate the ignorance on the parts of both managers and workers which led to unrealistic production targets and piece-rates of pay, and to inefficient ways of production.

Other classical theorists

Taylor was not the only proponent of scientific management. Other early supporters included Frank and Lillian Gilbreth and Henry Gantt.

THE GILBRETHS

The Gilbreths' contribution to scientific management was to develop motion study into a management tool capable of analysing work operations to establish the most efficient way of doing any particular task.

Frank Gilbreth (1917) defined motion study as 'dividing the work into the most fundamental elements possible; studying these elements separately and in relation to one another; and from these studied elements, when timed, building methods of least waste'.

Motion study was carried out using flow process charts. Symbols were used to analyse the processes of

- Operation
- Inspection
- Storage
- Transportation
- Delay

Unlike Taylor, who tended to think of pay as being the only motivator of workers and, therefore, that if workers were paid a fair piece-rate they would increase their productivity in order to maximize their earnings, the Gilbreths recognized that workforce output was dependent upon other factors as well. These included worker fatigue, poor lighting, heating and ventilation. The Gilbreths used motion studies to help reduce fatigue among workers, and they also introduced rest periods and shorter working days.

HENRY GANTT

Gantt was one of Taylor's colleagues. He, too, humanized Taylor's ideas of scientific management by introducing day-rates of pay (instead of the piece-rate system), with additional bonuses for those workers who exceeded the daily production targets. Foremen were also encouraged to train workers in their jobs by receiving a bonus for every worker who met the production targets.

Gantt is chiefly remembered today for developing a type of bar chart showing the time relationships between the stages in production processes. The Gantt chart (Figure 1.2) was originally designed to show how far a task had been achieved in comparison to the optimum target set.

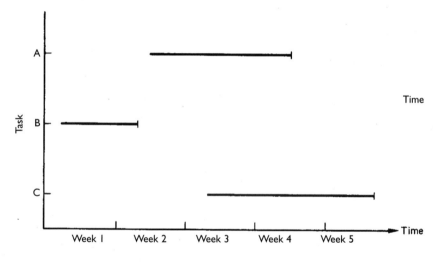

Figure 1.2 A Gantt chart

HENRI FAYOL (1841–1925)

Henri Fayol, a French industrialist, did more than anyone to popularize the idea of the 'universality of management principles': the concept that, regardless of the sort of business in question, the same broad principles of management apply. While Taylor's work was concentrated upon the shop-floor, Fayol studied management's role throughout the organization.

Fayol is known as the 'father of modern operational management theory', and, as you will see, his principles of management and his ideas on what the task of management entails are still very much in use.

FAYOL'S FUNCTIONS OF MANAGEMENT

Fayol identified five elements or functions of management (Figure 1.3): planning, organizing, commanding, coordinating and controlling.

1 *Planning*. Choosing objectives and the strategies, policies, and procedures for achieving them.
2 *Organizing*. Establishing a structure of tasks which have to be followed to achieve the organization's objectives, dividing these tasks up into jobs for individual employees, delegating authority, co-ordinating the work of different people, and setting up information and communication systems.
3 *Commanding*. Giving instructions and leadership to subordinates.
4 *Coordinating*. Harmonizing the work of different groups so that individuals are all working towards the common goals of the organization.
5 *Controlling*. Measuring, checking and correcting, if necessary, the results achieved, to ensure that they match the planned results.

Figure 1.3 Fayol's management functions

FAYOL'S PRINCIPLES OF MANAGEMENT

Fayol developed his fourteen management principles from these five functions:

1 *Division of work*. The specialization of tasks, which Fayol regarded as necessary to achieve greater efficiency and productivity.

2 *Authority and responsibility*. The right to issue commands comes from authority; responsibility for the work done is also related to this authority, and in fact arises out of it.

3 *Discipline*. Fayol felt that good superiors, at all levels in the organization, were required if there was to be good company discipline.

4 *Unity of command*. Ideally, employees should only receive instructions from one superior, right up to the organization's management hierarchy.

5 *Unity of direction*. Each group of activities with the same objective should have a single plan and a single manager in charge.

6 *Subordination*. The interest of the individual should be regarded as of lesser importance than the general interest.

7 *Remuneration*. Remuneration for work should be fair both to the employees and to the employer. This means that no one should have cause for discontent.

8 *Centralization*. This is the extent to which authority is concentrated or dispersed in an organization.

9 *Scalar chain*. The 'chain of superiors', according to Fayol, extending through an organization, which should not be departed from lightly; although it could be by-passed on occasions if it would harm the company to follow the chain too closely.

10 *Order*. People and work should be organized in an orderly fashion.

11 *Equity*. Managers should be fair in their dealings with employees and situations.

12 *Stability of tenure*. Fayol could not see how a manager whose promotion prospects, or job itself, were dependent upon short-term contract or salary reviews could be expected to do his job well. Instead, there should be a proper period of training and settling in, together with freedom from interference at all times.

13 *Initiative*. This should be encouraged to the full.

14 *Esprit de corps*. Managers should build up morale and a good team spirit among the workforce.

The achievements of the classical management school

You will, hopefully, have noticed how many of the ideas of people like Taylor and Fayol are still influencing production and management approaches today: the division of work into its smallest, simplest elements is still very widespread in mass-production, assembly-line industries. Work studies and time-and-motion studies are also widely used, and Fayol's management principles give a more than adequate summary of what management should be about.

The classical theorists helped to bring about a far more formal and rational approach to management than there had been before, and there is no doubt that the improvements aimed for in increased productivity and workers' pay were achieved.

However, the drawbacks of this approach were the de-skilling of the work, and the increase in the boring, repetitive nature of the tasks. These are problems which are still to be solved. The classical approach also saw workers as being rational economic beings, motivated only by money. Motor manufacturing has been a classic example where workers concentrated on one routine task. More recently, companies such as Toyota and Nissan have introduced task groups where workers concentrate on a number of tasks in an area.

The human relations school

While the classical management approach focused upon the structure of the organization, the human relations, or behavioural, school concentrates upon the people within the organization – their social needs, motivation and behaviour. The behavioural approach really began in earnest during the 1920s and 1930s, when it became clear that classical management theories were not preventing a fall in levels of production.

The first really influential writer on the behavioural approach was Elton Mayo (1880–1949), who studied productivity levels and working conditions at the Hawthorne plant of the Western Electric Company in Chicago, between 1927 and 1932. However, a few writers had begun thinking along similar lines earlier: a French sociologist, Emile Durkheim (1825–1917), recognized that groups of people tended to form their own values and norms of behaviour, and were able to subordinate the behaviour of individual group members to these collective values.

Mary Parker Follett (1868–1933) expanded on Durkheim's work, and saw how important it was for managers to understand how and why social groups formed, and to reconcile individual workers' needs with these group needs.

ELTON MAYO AND THE HAWTHORNE STUDIES

The Hawthorne studies proved conclusively that workers could become highly motivated simply by being part of a social/work group, and by being consulted by managers about changes in work practices, etc. However, these social groups were also capable of acting against the organization's interests by setting group norms of production levels and exerting pressure on group members to conform to these levels.

Other proponents of the behavioural management approach include Abraham Maslow, McGregor, Herzberg, and Rensis Likert. Their work will be discussed later when we look at the problems of motivating people.

The systems school of approach

Systems management theory developed during the 1950s and 1960s. The theory does not look at just one aspect of an organization, as the classical and behavioural approaches do, but attempts to explain the behaviour of the organization in terms of the complete entity – people, structure, environment and technology. The organization is seen as a collection of interrelated and interacting parts, which have to be viewed as a whole.

Systems are classed as being either open or closed. A closed system is self-supporting and does not interact with the environment in which it exists. Open systems, however, such as business organizations, do interact with their external environments. A business will receive inputs from its environment (e.g. people, finance, raw materials), which it will use to produce goods, to be sold back into the outside community (see Figure 1.4).

The contribution of systems theory

Systems theory has contributed to the development of management thinking in four major ways:

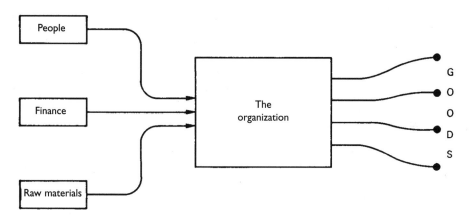

Figure 1.4   The organization as an open system

1 It has shown that managers have to consider all the elements which make up the organization – people, structure, technology, environment – as a cohesive whole, and not as separate items.
2 It has highlighted the influence that the external environment can have on the organization (something which has become more marked in recent years) precisely because open systems interact with this environment.
3 It has drawn attention to the importance of planning, because it has demonstrated how organizations have to

have a purpose or *raison d'être*, and thus how it is vital for managers to plan.

4 The success of any plan depends upon the monitoring of actual results against the planned results, and then correcting any deviations, i.e. control.

The contingency approach to management

The contingency management approach is a further development of the systems approach. The systems approach emphasizes the complex nature of the organization, with its different contributory variables; contingency theory takes the idea of the complex organization a few stages further on. According to the contingency approach, the style of management and the structure of an organization should reflect and change with changes in that organization's environment.

In contrast to all the other management theories we have looked at, contingency theory does not hold with the idea that there is only one best way of management, and that the principles of this can be applied under all circumstances. Instead, contingency theorists perhaps have a more realistic approach – that the most appropriate style of management will change over time, as the circumstances of the organization change, and that the right management approach for a particular problem will not necessarily be the correct approach for a different problem. To be really effective, managers should use whatever approach is best for the organization at that particular time.

The work of contingency theorists like Woodward, and Burns and Stalker, will be discussed in detail when the effects of factors such as company size, technology, etc., on the structure of organizations are looked at later.

SUMMARY

This chapter has, of necessity, been concerned with a great deal of theory. In it we have defined the management task as consisting of organizing groups of individuals so that they work together towards common goals or, in other words, deciding what has to be done and getting other people to do it.

We have seen how the management task is achieved through the processes of planning, making decisions, organizing, leading, motivating, communicating and controlling.

We have also looked at how management theories have developed over the years, from the one-dimensional classical (or scientific) and behavioural approaches, through to the multidimensional approach of the systems school, and finally to the contingency theorists' idea of flexible management.

Part Two
The
Management
Processes

2 Planning

The first process of the management task that we are going to look at is planning. Planning is essential not just for successful management, but for the success of almost every activity you can think of. Planning can be defined as deciding in advance what to do, how to do this particular task, when to do it, and who is to do it.

In the context of the management task, planning involves selecting strategies from different possible courses of action, not just for the enterprise as a whole but also for every department or section of it. This requires the organization to define its objectives, and for each department or section to set its own goals and targets in order to meet these objectives, and then to find ways to achieve these goals.

If managers do not plan to some degree, they would have no idea whether or not the organization was accomplishing its purpose. How can you tell if you have reached your destination if you don't know where you want to get to when you set out?

There are four reasons why planning is important for good management:

1 Planning helps to offset the effects of uncertainty and change, on the old principle that to be forewarned is to be forearmed. This is not to say that the planning process removes, or even lessens, the presence of risk; but planning does make managers more aware of the risks involved.

2 Planning focuses attention on the organization's real objectives.

3 Planning helps to make the operations of the organization more economical.

4 Planning aids the process of control, because managers have a benchmark against which they can measure the actual results achieved.

THE DIFFERENT TYPES OF PLANS

There are four different types or levels of planning. They differ from each other, firstly, in the time-scale that each level covers, and, secondly, in the amount of detail they contain. As a general rule, the longer the time-period covered by the plan, the less the detail contained in the plan, and the greater the degree of uncertainty and risk involved. It is also true that the longer the time-scale of the plan, the more senior are the managers who are involved in the planning process.

The relationships between these factors are illustrated below:

Plans	Time-scale	Degree of detail	Seniority of managers
Strategic	5–10 yrs	Vague	Board level
Management	12 mths	High	Department heads
Operational	1–4 wks	Very high	Junior managers

The overall coordination and implementation of these three levels of planning is usually referred to as *corporate planning*. As its name suggests, corporate planning is concerned with planning for the company as a whole, in order to ensure that the long-term objectives of each department are compatible and do not conflict either with each other, or with the ultimate goals of the organization. Figure 2.1 shows how each planning level dovetails together to form an organized whole.

Corporate planning

Peter Drucker defined corporate planning as:

> The continuous process of making present risk-taking decisions systematically and with the greatest knowledge of their futurity; organizing systematically the efforts needed to carry out these decisions, and measuring the results of these decisions against the expectations through organized, systematic feedback.

The purpose of planning on a corporate basis is to define and clarify the goals of the organization as a whole. It involves making appraisals of the organization's major strengths and weaknesses, and considering the external opportunities and threats posed by the organization's environment. These will all affect which goals the organization will be able, realistically, to achieve.

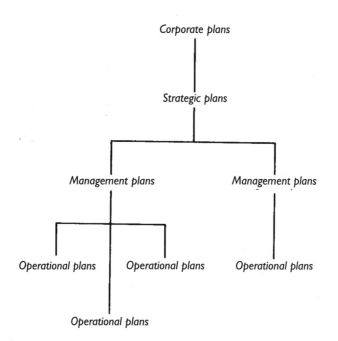

Figure 2.1   The different planning levels in an organization

Corporate planning also involves transforming long-term strategies into suffi-
ciently detailed medium-term and operational plans (which can be changed if
necessary) to help to ensure that the organization's overall objectives are
achieved.

WHY CORPORATE PLANNING IS NECESSARY

A system of corporate planning, involving the coordination of plans for the
entire business over a period of several years, is necessary for several reasons:

1 The importance that the real objectives of an organization
   are identified cannot be emphasized enough, and that, these
   having been identified, the whole business works towards
   them using co-ordinated strategies. A business with dis-
   parate goals will, at best, not perform as successfully as it
   could and, at worst, will tear itself apart. You can imagine
   the difficulties generated within conglomerates if organizations like Hanson did not have cohesive objectives.
2 The degree of competition for finite resources within an
   organization increases with the size of the organization, and
   this creates a need for central planning and control, rather
   than planning by individual departments or managers.
3 The ever-quickening pace of change means that organiza-

tions have to adapt and react to change *corporately* to survive, rather than on an individual departmental basis.

Strategic planning

Strategic planning is the long-range planning part of the corporate planning process. It involves establishing where the organization wants to be in five or ten years' time; where it is actually likely to be, in view of any forecast changes in its business environment; and developing long-term plans to bridge any possible gaps between where it wants to go, and where it looks like ending up.

Examples of long-term strategies are the development of new products, the opening up of new markets, and the expansion into different areas of business.

Management planning

This is a lower, intermediate level of planning. Management planning is concerned with, for example, the following areas:

1 Determining the structure of the organization.
2 Establishing functional and departmental objectives and targets, in line with the strategic plans and aims.
3 Deciding upon product/sales mixes.
4 Setting budgets, and planning staff requirements.

Operational planning

The lowest level of planning is that of operational planning, covering weekly and day-to-day planning. It involves the line manager and management at supervisory and foreman levels in setting specific tasks and key targets to help to achieve the relevant management plan. Some of these targets are expressed in financial terms; others are expressed in measures such as output per employee, the percentage utilization of machines, cost levels, etc. Once these targets have been set, they should be monitored and revised as necessary. If revisions are made in these short-term targets, then the whole plan should be altered accordingly, so that the long-term perspective is maintained but the entire plan is kept up to date.

THE PLANNING CYCLE

The successful operation of most organizations is based upon planning. This does not just happen, however. It results from a systematic process, which can be a lengthy and thought-provoking exercise. The process involved in corporate planning is designed so that organizations can establish the following:

1 What their main objectives are, and just why and for what purpose they exist.

2 What opportunities and threats are presented by their external environment.

3 What their own internal strengths and weaknesses are, especially in relation to the external environment they operate
in.

4 A sound base for their strategic and operational planning.

5 Policies which will allow their employees to follow and
achieve the companies' objectives.

The planning process consists of several stages, and these are shown in
Figure 2.2.

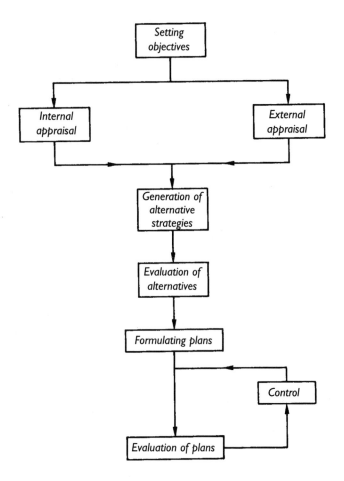

Figure 2.2   The stages in the planning cycle

Setting objectives

The first stage in the planning process is the identification and description of the organization's objectives. The importance of this step cannot be overstated. Objectives are the ends towards which the activities of an organization are directed; they give purpose and meaning to the organization's existence. For example, for a public service such as The Post Office, the primary purpose of the organization would be 'to provide a service for the community'.

There are two types of objectives. The first type includes those that lay down the overall purpose of the organization (as above). The second type includes those that set out the organization's long-term aims, defining what sort of organization it intends to be in the future, and what kind of business the organization expects to be conducting.

The traditional overall objective for businesses is to maximize profits. However, this is a rather unrealistic aim, not least because it is almost impossible to judge whether or not the company has maximized its profits! A project which was not undertaken might have yielded greater returns than one chosen in its place; there is very little way of telling for sure. Maximizing profits in the short term may also reduce shareholders' returns over a longer period.

This traditional maximization of profits objective, therefore, is usually amended to the achievement of sufficient profits to ensure the company's survival and growth, and to give shareholders an acceptable return on their investment.

Cyert and March (1963) have put forward the behavioural, or stakeholder, theory of the firm. According to this, the organization is made up of a coalition of different interest groups, or stakeholders: managers, employees, shareholders, customers, suppliers, and so on. Therefore, the organization's long-term objectives are set to cover a wide variety of areas (such as market share, sales growth, public responsibility, etc.), in order to satisfy the diverse interests of these different groups. The reason why these different objectives have to be set is due to the fact that the owners of modern companies are often not the same people who control businesses in practice, because of the emergence of multiple shareholders (who are often themselves other corporate bodies) and professional managers. However, the different objectives still have to be compatible, because an organization cannot successfully operate while heading in opposite directions.

Frequently set objectives

Peter Drucker, in *The Practice of Management*, outlines seven areas in which the majority of organizations establish objectives in order to try and satisfy the differing interests of each group of stakeholders. These objectives cover the organization's profitability, market share and standing, productivity, management and employee performance, technical innovation, social responsibility, and resource management.

1 *Profitability*. The primary goal of any profit-making business has to be growth in its earnings per share ratio. When planning long-term strategies for earnings growth, aspects such as net dividends, taxation, profit and inflation have to be considered. Non-profit-making organizations, such as charities and public services, while not having to produce earnings for shareholders, still have either to keep within a budget or to generate sufficient net profit to fund their activities. Thus both these sorts of organization have to set profit-related goals.

2 *Market share and standing*. Corporate marketing objectives can cover areas such as what products are to be sold in which markets; whether or not the organization should aim to be a market leader in terms of pricing or product development; what degree of market penetration it should seek; and the standards of service required.

3 *Productivity*. Productivity is very important for an organization, as productivity and profitability are closely linked. Productivity objectives are normally expressed in terms of output per employee, and output in relation to plant, material yields, and costs.

4 *Management and employee performance*. Many businesses set objectives covering the development of good management/ employee relations, workforce training and development, and future management structure. Management performance is covered a little later in this chapter in the section on management by objectives.

5 *Technical innovation*. The company has to decide whether or not it should aim to be a technical innovator in terms of its products, or whether it will follow the lead set by others. The organization's ability to be an innovator depends upon the technical and creative resources at its disposal. However, a technical policy should be devised, and objectives for research and development (or just development) set, in conjunction with the company's marketing and manufacturing objectives. Schmidt plc, a manufacturer of street cleaning equipment, includes in its objectives the wish to be at the forefront of technology in the industry and, to achieve this, to allocate 12 per cent of turnover to research and development.

6 *Social and public responsibility*. Organizations are increasingly setting objectives covering their social responsibilities, such as the preservation and improvement of the environment, consumer protection objectives, improvements in working conditions, and sponsorship and participation in local community activities. Unilever sets as one objective 'to

contribute to a cleaner environment'. Many organizations, such as Shell, British Gas and Saab, use these objectives as part of their marketing policy.

7 *Resource utilization.* Many organizations set objectives which relate to the efficient use of physical and financial resources.

Whatever objectives are set by the organization, they must be specific goals, which the senior management team can translate into plans and strategies for action.

> **INVESTIGATE**
>
> Take a few minutes just to think about your own company, department, or an organization you are familiar with, and note down what you see as its objectives, under each of the above headings.

Internal appraisal

The purpose of an internal business appraisal is to allow the organization to identify just which functions it is good at, and which functions it is less successful at undertaking. This should enable the organization to forecast what might be the results in a few years' time if it continues as it is, without reducing its weaknesses and capitalizing on its strengths, i.e. a 'steady as she goes' strategy. The areas which should be examined include the following:

1 *Product mix.* The range of the company's products, together with their age, quality, and the durability of their appeal to customers, together with the company's pricing policy and competitiveness compared with rival products, should all be analysed. The company's record of introducing successful new products is also very important, especially if the company is relying upon a few elderly successful products for a large proportion of its profits.

2 *Markets.* The range of markets that the company sells its products in, as well as market share and growth rate, and the composition of each market by customer type, geographical area, and so on. If an organization is very reliant upon one particular section of the population for its market, it might consider broadening its appeal, just as Radio 2 has tried to attract younger listeners as its traditional 'market' ages.

3 *Production and supply.* The company should analyse trends in output compared to production capacity; productivity levels; the quality of finished products; wastage and spoilage

rates; whether its raw material suppliers are efficient in terms of delivery times, quality, etc., or not; the efficiency of stock control methods, and so on.

4 *Research and development.* The organization's R&D policy should be compared with that of its competitors, in terms of its appropriateness for the company, its success rate in developing new products and processes, etc.

5 *Finance.* The company's finances should be examined in terms of present and projected performance, compared with past performance trends and inter-firm or industrial averages, in order to show the relative strength of the company. The effectiveness of routine financial reporting, budgeting and controls should also be looked at.

6 *Personnel.* The age, ability and skills of the company's workforce should be analysed in terms of overall productivity, together with such matters as the adequacy of staff training, and the state of industrial relations.

7 *Management.* Again, the age, ability and skills of the company's management team should be examined, plus management recruitment and promotion policies, and especially the provisions for succession to senior management posts.

8 *Organizational structure.* The suitability of the organization's structure for the company's business, for example the channels of communication, the lines of authority, the degree of independence given to managers to act, etc.

It is very important that an internal appraisal is an objective exercise, which does not seek to apportion blame for past mistakes. Constructive ideas for solving problems are obviously far more helpful than recriminations and office political point-scoring.

Having said that, it is also important that any appraisal is an honest and thorough one. The key to this is the questioning of the reasons behind every action, i.e. the vital thing is to ask just *why* something is done, and not to accept 'it's always been done this way' as a proper answer without any close examination.

INVESTIGATE

Using the appropriate areas outlined above, jot down the strengths and weaknesses of your company department, or college, as you see them.

External appraisal

An appraisal of the organization's external business environment is the counterpart of the internal appraisal. Such an external appraisal reviews the developments in the outside world in which the organization exists, and tries to forecast possible changes in it which could pose either a serious threat to the company (in which case it can take action to lessen the impact), or opportunities which can be exploited for the good of the business (Figure 2.3).

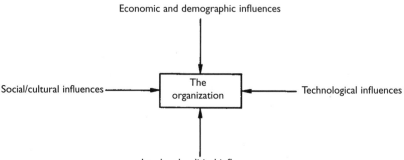

Figure 2.3   Environmental influences on the organization

The business environment is covered in more detail in Part Four; here we will just look briefly at some of those areas within the outside environment which the organization should examine during an external appraisal.

1 *The economic environment.* An organization which conducts its business exclusively in one country will need to focus on its domestic economy, while a multinational company will have to assess the international economic situation. However, both will need to collect and assess information which is relevant to their marketing plans, for example changes in the gross domestic product, changes in fixed capital information requirements, changes in consumer income and expenditure, inflation forecasts, the opening up of the European Community markets, etc.

2 *The political environment.* An organization will have to assess the political environment within which it operates, in terms of its stability and how political decisions will affect the organization's business. For example, a company operating in Hong Kong will need to review and take into consideration the uncertain political future of that place when forming its plans. On a more mundane level, an appraisal of the political environment should include such areas as government action in terms of taxation and business subsidies, spending, import duties, and the possible effects of a change of government.

3 *The legal environment.* The external appraisal will also have to examine the legal environment. The organization will be affected to some degree by, for example, the legal changes resulting from the establishment of the single European market, relating to competition rules, patents, the sale of goods, pollution controls, working regulations and industrial standards. The change to the law on Sunday trading in the UK, and the EU ban on tobacco advertising, are both examples of how the legal environment affects organizations.

4 *The social environment.* Closely linked to the political and legal environments is the social environment, because it is often thanks to pressure from certain social groups that politicians bring in new laws and regulations. The social environment has been affecting companies more and more recently, and changes in consumer tastes and perceptions can have a major impact on a business. For example, the growing awareness of environmental matters has led to many companies having to alter their production processes and images radically. Future changes in demographic trends and in the physical make-up of the population (with the increase in numbers of pensioners and decrease in people of working age) will also affect companies in varying degrees.

5 *The technological environment.* Technological factors, i.e. changes in the supply of raw materials, production methods, and new product developments, need to be considered especially carefully in an external appraisal, because of the speed with which changes in technology are occurring.

INVESTIGATE

As with the section on internal appraisal, take a few minutes to think what threats and opportunities to your organization are posed by the external environment, and how any threats could be minimized and opportunities taken advantage of.

Clearly, the importance of each environment type varies according to the industry concerned. The social environment, will be particularly important to BAT Industries plc with significant tobacco investments, whereas the technological environment will be crucial to Amstrad Electronics.

Any external appraisal not only must examine the present situation within the environment and its on-going changes, but it should also try to assess any likely changes in the future. Such forecasting of likely environmental change is often little better than intelligent guesswork, due to the unpredictable nature of many different variables and events. However, the widespread use of computer technology to create models and 'most likely' scenarios, through the manipulation of large amounts of data, has made it easier for companies to make reasonable predictions. But it should be remembered that forecasting environmental changes will help to reduce some of the risk involved; however, uncertainty will always be present in the planning process.

Both internal and external appraisals should be concerned with identifying the few areas considered to be crucial for the organization's success or failure over the coming five or ten years. The identification of the major strengths and weaknesses of the business, and the opportunities and threats posed by its environment, is sometimes referred to as SWOT analysis.

Evaluation of alternatives

The next stage in the planning process is to choose and evaluate the possible strategies which will make the most of the organization's strengths and the business opportunities presented to it by its external environment, while correcting any major weaknesses and minimizing external threats to its survival. Hopefully, different ideas will have presented themselves during the SWOT analysis, and usually the problem is not in the generation of alternative plans, but in the reduction of the alternatives to a manageable number of those promising to be the most fruitful for the business!

The internal and external appraisals may also have thrown up a fairly large number of problems and opportunities; in this situation it is obviously better for the organization to rate them in terms of their urgency and importance and to concentrate on the three or four most vital ones.

The possible alternatives have to be examined to establish just what their effects will be on the company. They should be evaluated in terms of whether or not the company will be better off if the particular idea is adopted than if no change were made; the effect of the change on the organization's profits year by year; and whether or not the organization would be able to raise sufficient funding to meet all the anticipated expenditure required under the scheme.

The alternatives, of course, must also be evaluated in terms of meeting the organization's objectives. But it has to be borne in mind that the organization will have several objectives, and that fulfilling one objective may create constraints for the other objectives. Therefore, the organization may have to rank its objectives in order of their importance, and in the case of a clash of interests, a proposal which helps to fulfil an important objective should be chosen in preference to one which only fulfils lesser objectives.

There are three reasons why organizations do not evaluate possible alternatives in sufficient depth:

1 The large number of available alternatives often makes the task very daunting.
2 The amount of time needed for proper, detailed evaluations is regarded as excessive.

3 The uncertainty inherent in forecasting is assumed to make any detailed evaluation pointless.

However, if the alternatives are not considered properly, it invalidates the whole planning process.

The need to consider different ways of achieving given objectives on a regular basis is, generally, most keenly felt by private sector organizations, whose markets are under constant threat from competitors. However, the need also exists in the public sector, especially now that budget constraints require all managers to make the most efficient use of the resources under their control.

Formulating plans

When the different alternatives have been evaluated properly against the criteria set by the organization, and a specific course of action chosen, the point is reached at which broad strategies have to be translated into detailed plans. It is now that the implications for the various parts of the organization are made clear: specific year-by-year targets for each division and department are laid down, perhaps with an indication of the reasons for any changes from current targets; and the resources available to meet those targets are set out.

Plans vary greatly in the degree of detail contained in them. Some private sector organizations, such as the electronics group GEC, lay down financial targets for each individual company within the group, and then give the subsidiaries considerable freedom as to the strategies they adopt to meet those targets. However, at the other end of the spectrum, public sector organizations tend to be much more restricted in the policies which have to be adopted and the resources available to each division, with detailed budgets being set for equipment, materials, staff, etc.

The elements of commercial business plans tend to be made up in terms of particular products for various markets, and will lay down the resources required in order to implement them. The plans may include areas such as image as well as products and markets, although these latter factors usually dominate.

The coordination of short- and long-range plans

As we have seen, the strategic part of an organization's corporate plan will give a broad outline of the policies which the company intends to adopt in order to achieve its objectives. These policies are then broken down into management and operational plans, together with the establishment of key targets. It is often at this stage of the planning process that a serious error is made, in that these shorter-range plans are frequently made without reference to the long-range plans.

The integration of these long- and short-range plans is extremely important. No short-range target should be set unless it contributes to the achievement of the relevant long-range plan and overall corporate objectives. Sometimes, short-range decisions not only fail to do this, but actually impede, or require changes in, the company's strategic plans. It is part of the manager's job to consider immediate decisions and judge whether or not they contribute to the organization's long-range plans. Managers throughout the organization should be briefed regularly on its long-term plans and objectives, so that they can make decisions which are consistent with these aims.

Evaluation and control

The final stage of the planning process is that of evaluation and control. This involves the following:

1 Establishing performance targets.
2 Comparing the actual results achieved with these performance targets.
3 Analysing any deviations in the results from the acceptable tolerance limits.
4 Implementing any necessary modifications.

Effective evaluation and control needs an efficient monitoring procedure, which measures the extent of progress towards the fulfilment of set targets, and produces reports for the managers concerned with the relevant results and information, so that any problems can be remedied quickly.

Planning can be regarded as a closed loop system (Figure 2.4), with feedback on the results of the plans used to update them if necessary, and to check on their progress. Plans should never be so sacred that they cannot be changed and adapted if managers see fit.

MANAGEMENT BY OBJECTIVES

Some of you may well be familiar with the idea of 'management by objectives', and, indeed, may be working in organizations which use such a system of management. The phrase was first used by Peter Drucker in the 1950s; management by objectives was one of his principles of management.

Both Drucker and John Humble (another advocate of management by objectives) see the process as a way of coordinating and integrating the short- and long-term plans of the organization with the goals of junior and senior managers, and the need of individual managers to be able to contribute directly to the organization's success. Drucker comments that often a common organizational target is very difficult to aim at:

> in the business enterprise managers are not automatically directed towards a common goal. On the contrary, business, by its very nature, contains three powerful factors of misdirection: in the specialised work of most managers; in the hierarchical structure of management, and in the difference in vision and work and the resultant insulation of various levels of management.

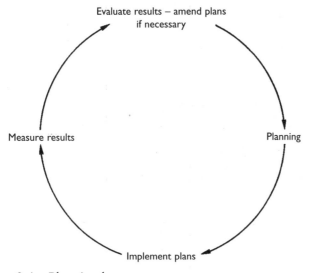

Figure 2.4   Planning loop system

The MBO process

Under the MBO process, the jobs of managers are analysed to establish the key areas where results are necessary. Then a list of key tasks which have to be performed is drawn up from these key areas. This list normally consists of no more than eight or nine tasks, and it should be drawn up jointly by the individual managers concerned and their superiors.

The list of key tasks is used to establish certain short-term goals which are the focus for immediate priority action by each manager. Each task is given a performance standard against which attainment can be measured over a set period. These standards are either quantitative (e.g. the sales of product X should be increased by 15% over the coming year), or qualitative (e.g. the report on Y should be acceptable to the Board). Usually, control data for each task are also specified. These are sources of information against which the fulfilling of the set standards can be checked. In the first example above, the control data would be the relevant sales figures for the year.

At the end of the period, the results of the tasks should be reviewed in order to assess the manager's performance. Again, this review should be carried out jointly by both the manager concerned and the manager's superior. This allows individuals to gauge how well they are doing their jobs, and allows realistic discussions between them and their superiors about their progress and achievements. Management by objectives also allows standards and specific targets to be set for managers who do not have obviously quantifiable jobs.

The advantages of management by objectives

Management by objectives has several advantages for organizations:

1 It forces managers to think of planning for results, rather than merely planning work; this is very important, because only results-orientated planning makes any sense.
2 It increases commitment throughout the company to the aims of the organization, because everyone should be working towards definite targets which are all well coordinated.
3 It forces companies to clarify their internal structures and organizational roles.
4 It helps in the development of effective control systems, as well as leading to more effective planning.

Problems with management by objectives

1 A common cause of problems with MBO is due to senior managers not spending enough time teaching and explaining the system and the ideas behind it to the rest of the organization.
2 There is often a failure to give adequate guidelines to those managers setting their subordinates' objectives. Managers have to know what the corporate goals are and how their tasks fit in with them.
3 Another problem with MBO is that short-term targets are usually set, which risks emphasizing short-term at the expense of long-range planning.
4 Problems can arise in setting up a system that cannot adapt quickly to changes within and outside the organization. Although targets may cease to be meaningful if they are changed too often, it is none the less unwise to expect a manager to work towards a target that has been made obsolete by revised corporate objectives or changes in the environment.

WHY PLANNING SYSTEMS CAN FAIL

It is obvious that planning systems can fail. The reasons for such failure are summarized briefly below:

1 The single most important reason for the failure of planning systems is a lack of commitment to the planning process, particularly among an organization's senior management.
2 Resistance to change among middle and junior management and among the ordinary workforce.

3 The failure to set meaningful, verifiable targets, and the absence of clear aims for the business as a whole.

4 The failure to appreciate the scope of the plans and the all-encompassing nature of the planning system.

5 Over-reliance on past experiences: it is not always true that what was done in the past is likely to be appropriate in future situations.

6 Poor and inflexible control techniques. Planning cannot be effective unless those people responsible for the system know how well it is working.

7 A hostile external environment, i.e. a period of change so rapid as to require constant adjustment to plans, without it ever being possible to achieve identifiable results.

8 A lack of clear delegation in the organization. It is very difficult for people to plan if they do not know what their jobs are and how these relate to others in the organization. A lack of clear lines of authority also makes it difficult to take decisions.

HOW PLANNING SYSTEMS CAN BE EFFECTIVE

Planning systems can be effective, however, if senior management establish a favourable climate for planning. At each level of management targets must be set, managers must be involved in the planning process throughout, reviews must be made of subordinates' plans and performances, and checks must be made to ensure that people have appropriate assistance and information. An organization's senior management team is the single most important factor in determining the success or failure of the planning system, and so the team must be committed to the planning process. Good organization is also needed; in any business which plans effectively, planning and doing are not separated.

Communication is also a vital part of planning. If planning is to be effective the goals, strategies and policies of the organization have to be communicated. Otherwise, the planning process becomes uncoordinated and flounders.

A lack of communication can create what is known as a planning gap. In this situation the senior management understands the organization's goals and the plans; the workforce knows what it has to do each day; but the middle-level managers do not understand how their departmental goals and policies tie in with those of the organization as a whole. Effective planning is fostered when managers are given the opportunity to contribute to the plans which affect their particular areas of authority.

SUMMARY

In this chapter we have looked at the reasons why planning is so important for *all* organizations, and how a systematic, coordinated planning process can make the difference between an average business and a successful one.

We have seen that there are four different types of planning – corporate, strategic, management and operational – each of which covers a different time-span, involves different degrees of detail and uncertainty, and is carried out at different management levels.

The stages in a systematic planning process have been examined in detail, together with some of the reasons why corporate planning can fail, and what steps can be taken by managers to help to ensure its success.

The vital ingredient for a successful system of planning is the active support and backing of the senior management team in general, and the chief executive in particular, because such a system affects the entire organization and requires that everyone works towards common, well-communicated objectives and goals.

CHECKLIST: CHAPTER 2

After this chapter you will be able to identify:

1 Four types/levels of planning:
- Corporate plans
- Strategic plans
- Management plans
- Operational plans

2 That corporate planning should establish:
- Objectives
- Opportunities and threats in external environment
- Strengths and weaknesses
- A sound base for strategic operational planning
- Policies to enable objectives to be achieved

3 The planning cycle:
- Setting objectives
- Internal/external appraisal
- Alternative strategies
- Evaluate alternatives
- Formulate plans
- Evaluate plans

4 Management by objectives:
- Managers' jobs analysed to identify key areas where results are needed
- The advantages and disadvantages of MBO

5 Planning failures:
- Lack of commitment
- Resistance to change
- Poor target setting

3 Decision-making

Decision-making – that process of thought and action that leads to a decision – lies at the heart of management. Managers spend their time choosing between alternative courses of action on the basis of the information available to them at the time; in other words, making decisions.

Decision-making is closely linked with the management process of planning, which we have just looked at. Planning is all about taking decisions about future actions. Indeed, Ackoff (1970) writes that planning is in fact a particular type of decision-making, with three distinguishing characteristics:

1 It is anticipatory decision-making. Planning 'is a process of deciding what to do and how to do it before action is required'. Because it takes time to decide what to do it is necessary to plan ahead.
2 Planning involves a set of interdependent decisions. This set of decisions is often too large to handle all at once, and therefore is better dealt with in stages. Decisions made in the earlier stages will affect later decisions, and vice versa; it may sometimes be necessary to alter an earlier decision in the light of decisions taken later on.
3 Planning is directed towards making decisions which would not otherwise be made.

Just as in the planning process, different levels of management have to make different types of decisions, with differing amounts of risk and uncertainty attached to them, and which are of differing time-spans.

Supervisors and junior levels of management have (usually!) fairly clear-cut decisions to make, where the problems and their solutions are routine. Decisions made at this level normally have to be made quickly. The resulting success or failure of such decisions is also quickly apparent. The time-span is short, and there is usually little uncertainty associated with this level of decision-making.

However, as managers progress up the organizational hierarchy, the decisions they have to make result in longer and longer gaps between the problems being noted and the results of their decisions becoming known. Decisions are also subject to more and more uncertainty and risk, and the consequences of wrong decisions become more and more costly. You will find that, often, senior managers delegate some problems to their subordinates in order to prepare them for this type of decision-making.

In this chapter we will look at some of the theories behind decision-making, and then go on to examine the decision-making process. Finally, we will briefly discuss some of the techniques used to analyse and evaluate possible solutions to problems.

THEORIES OF DECISION-MAKING

There are two main schools of thought underlying the decision-making process: the classical theory and the behavioural theories of writers such as Simon and Cyert and March.

The classical theory of decision-making

The classical theory of rational, economic decision-making assumes that the decision-maker:

1 Has complete knowledge of all the possible alternative courses of action.
2 Has complete knowledge of the consequences of taking every alternative.
3 Can attach definite payoffs to each possible outcome.
4 Can put each payoff in order, from the highest to the lowest payoff.

Obviously, these assumptions are fairly unrealistic and are rarely valid because of various factors, such as the following:

1 Uncertainty – possible alternative courses of action may not be known or identifiable; and the outcomes and payoffs of any individual course of action may also be uncertain.
2 The decision-maker may have many criteria, both quantifiable and unquantifiable, by which he or she wishes to value a possible course of action, and not merely the monetary payoff.

3 There may be practical limitations on the analysis of the courses of action. The decision-maker may lack the mental capacity to evaluate and compare all the possible alternatives. A search for, and evaluation of, all possible alternatives is also usually impracticable, because of the limited time and resources which can normally be devoted to any one problem.

The behavioural theory of decision-making

It was Simon (1957) who put forward the idea of 'administrative man' as a more realistic alternative to the 'rational, economic man' of the classical theorists. 'Administrative man' is a satisficer rather than a perfectionist, and his decision-making behaviour can be summed up as follows:

1 When choosing between alternatives, decision-makers look for a scheme which provides a satisfactory payoff, not the best possible payoff.
2 Decision-makers recognize that their perception of the world is only a very simplified model of the real world.
3 A satisficer can make a choice without first determining all the possible alternatives, and without ascertaining that these are actually all the alternatives.

Satisficing decisions

Simon proposed that satisficers simplify the decision-making process in various ways, in order to define the decision within the bounds of their mental capacities. In this way decision-makers limit their search to the identification of a course of action that merely satisfies some minimum set of requirements. This does not mean that large numbers of alternative schemes are not examined, but the alternatives are examined sequentially, and the first satisfactory one to be evaluated is usually the alternative selected.

THE DECISION-MAKING PROCESS

There are several steps in the decision-making process:

1 The problem must be defined – this involves diagnosing the *real* problem and not just the symptoms of it, as well as distinguishing between conditions which are 'musts' and conditions which are 'shoulds'. For example, a staffing problem can be analysed as 'We *must* employ someone who can do the job at the given salary, and they *should* fit in well with others in the organization'.
2 The relevant facts have to be gathered together and analysed

– this involves finding out which people have the most experience of the problem and the most information about it.

3 Develop alternative solutions – this is a natural extension to the previous stage of fact gathering, and many possible solutions will arise naturally from it. A number of solutions should really be examined, rather than the first feasible one being chosen. This can be viewed as a compromise between the extremes of both satisficing and economic decision-making.

4 Evaluate the alternative solutions – in terms of solving the original problem and meeting the organization's overall objectives.

5 Select the best alternative – the choice will be based on the available information and will usually be a compromise solution. Drucker (1955) suggests four factors which should be used to judge potential solutions:
   (a) the risk involved compared to the expected gain;
   (b) the amount of effort that each alternative involves;
   (c) the time-span involved with each alternative; this is especially important if dramatic changes are needed immediately; and
   (d) the availability of any additional resources which may be required.

6 Analyse the possible consequences of the decision – this is important so that any anticipated problems can be dealt with successfully. For example, there may be resistance to change within the organization, or additional funding may have to be raised.

7 Implement the decision – this will involve setting up a budget and defining responsibilities to ensure the project's completion. There will also need to be a system of checking and control to ensure that the decision is implemented correctly.

Decision-making and problem-solving

As we have seen, decision-making is closely linked to the management task of planning. It is obviously also similar to the task of problem-solving. Problem-solving and decision-making are not actually the same, although you may be forgiven for thinking that they are!

Luthans (1981) describes problem-solving as 'any goal-directed activity that must overcome some type of barrier to accomplish the goal'. Problem-solving is thus a more extensive activity than decision-making, and it is usually the need to solve a problem that creates the need for a decision. Unfortunately, in problem-solving the emphasis is too often placed exclusively on obtaining answers, when it is just as important to be sure that the right problem has been identified!

Steps in the problem-solving process

Elbing (1980) describes the management task of problem-solving as a five-step process:

1 The manager perceives a problem, perhaps without a clear, rational reason for doing so.
2 The manager responds by attempting to find out the causes of the problem.
3 In addition, the manager must attempt to define the nature of the problem.
4 The manager must select a solution, which will involve making a decision.
5 The implementation of the chosen course of action, whether or not it actually leads to a solution of the problem.

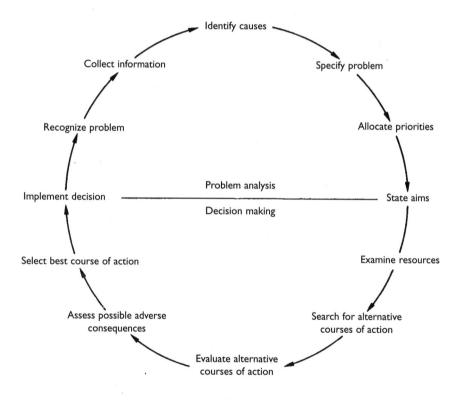

Figure 3.1   Steps in problem analysis and decision-making

Figure 3.1 shows how the stages involved in decision-making and problem-solving combine to form a seamless process.

The steps in decision-making

1 *Statement of aims.* It is very necessary to have a clear understanding of what needs to be achieved, or what the real,
underlying problem is, particularly when a number of managers are involved in the decision-making. A simple example
of the importance of identifying the underlying problem is
that of the driver who notices that her car is low on oil.
Topping it up may solve the immediate problem, but only
temporarily if there is an oil leak, and the latter could (if it
isn't fixed) result in serious engine damage.

2 *Examination of resources.* Any consideration of the available resources should cover the three critical areas of:

(a) people – who is available to help; who has experience
and training which could help; how many people are
available to do any extra work involved?

(b) finances – what can be spent on the project, and the
limits of financial authority?

(c) materials and equipment – where can the work be done;
the availability of raw materials; does any specialized
equipment need to be used, and if so, is such equipment
available?

3 *Searching for alternatives.* Some guidelines are suggested
below which may help when alternative courses of action
are being looked for:

(a) make use of any knowledge and experience which is
already available; ready-made solutions often already
exist, written up in reports; a little digging around in the
appropriate journals can save a considerable amount of
time and money later on.

(b) ask penetrating questions, don't just accept things at
their face value.

(c) apply creative, lateral thinking.

4 *Evaluation of alternatives.* Evaluating the alternative solutions involves, to begin with, assessing how well each meets
the desired end. The next part is concerned with assessing
the advantages and disadvantages of each possible solution
against one another to arrive at a balanced final decision.
There are a number of techniques which can be used to evaluate alternatives. These are discussed later on in this chapter.

5 *Selecting the best course of action.* Although we can trace a
sequence of logical thought processes through each stage of
decision-making, at the moment of decision the logic may
not be clear. The manager will, in effect, be putting a value
on those factors which cannot be formally evaluated and
which may, therefore, have been omitted from the earlier

steps in the process. The mark of a good manager is 'flair' – that innate sense, possibly developed through long experience, of the illogicalities in human behaviour and of the element of chance in the business environment.

6 *Implementation.* A decision has no value to the business; indeed, it might be said that for all practical purposes it does not exist, until it has been put into effect. The true test of confidence in the decision-making process comes when the decision has to be converted into a plan of action; it is then that money, people and other resources are committed. A systematic approach to the whole process of problem analysis and decision-making is essential if only for this purpose – to give managers enough confidence in the decision to initiate action.

CRITERIA FOR GOOD DECISION-MAKING

Perhaps the most serious difficulty in decision-making is the existence of objectives and aims which cannot be quantified. Janis and Mann (1977) recognized this problem and suggested making the assumption that a decision is likely to be more satisfactory when the quality of the decision-making procedure is high. They set out seven major criteria which can be used to help determine whether or not the decision-making process is of a high quality:

1 The identification of a wide range of alternative courses of action.
2 Consideration of the full range of objectives used and the values implied by this choice.
3 A careful consideration of the costs and risks of both the positive and negative consequences of each alternative.
4 A diligent search for new information for the further evaluation of possible solutions.
5 The acceptance of any new information, even when it does not support the course of action initially preferred.
6 The re-examination of the positive and negative consequences of all known alternatives, before making a final choice.
7 Making detailed plans for implementing the chosen course of action, including contingency plans in the event of various known risks actually occurring.

Janis and Mann use the term 'vigilant information processing' (VIP) to describe a decision process where all seven criteria have been met to the best of the decision-maker's ability.

DECISION ANALYSIS TECHNIQUES

There are many techniques for evaluating possible solutions, ranging from the fairly simple to complex mathematically-based techniques. The ones outlined below are some of the more common ones in use.

Marginal or incremental costing

Marginal costing compares the additional revenues which are forecasted to be generated by each possible scheme with the forecasted costs of each. It is a useful technique because it emphasizes variables instead of constants and averages. However, the drawback of marginal costing is that it can be very difficult to quantify adequately the benefits which may result from a project (especially if the project under consideration is a long-term, radical one) and all the costs which could be incurred.

Discounted cash flow appraisal

Discounted cash flow (DCF) methods of appraisal are probably the most widely used analysis techniques. They are based on the assumption that money which is received now is worth more than money which is received at some point in the future. This is because of factors such as inflation, and because cash received now can earn interest in the intervening period.

    The two main methods of DCF appraisal are finding a project's net present value (NPV), and calculating its internal rate of return (IRR). Calculating the NPV involves discounting all the project's forecasted future net cash flows to their present value. The IRR of a project is the discount rate which gives an NPV of zero. In investment terms, if the IRR of a project is greater than the firm's cost of capital, then it is worth undertaking. When used to evaluate possible schemes, both methods enable projects' profitabilities over the course of their lifetimes to be compared.

Cost–benefit analysis

This evaluation technique is used when the data involved cannot be quantified, but when things like the social benefits and costs of a possible project (such as pollution or unemployment) are important in making the decision. Cost–benefit analysis works by weighing the effectiveness of each alternative in meeting the scheme's objectives against its potential costs. The major drawback of the method is its subjectiveness. However, cost–benefit analysis can be very useful, especially if used together with other, more objective, appraisal techniques.

Sensitivity analysis

Sensitivity analysis questions the assumptions behind each possible plan to see how valid they are. The dependence of the plan on each assumption is also assessed, in order to find out what degree of risk is being taken, and on how sound a basis. For example, a project which depends on a certain sum being raised by a share issue for its success should be reassessed if the probability of such a sum being raised is low. Sensitivity analysis has the advantage of being easy to use, especially with computer spreadsheet packages.

Risk analysis

Risk analysis gauges the range of each variable in a project and the probability of it occurring, for example the chances of the cost exceeding or falling below the best estimate, and by how much.

Decision tree analysis

Decision trees (such as the one shown in Figure 3.2) are conceptual maps of sequences of possible decisions and their outcomes. When the probability of each outcome occurring is added to the tree, the riskiness of each course of action can be assessed, and the possible payoffs from each can be calculated.

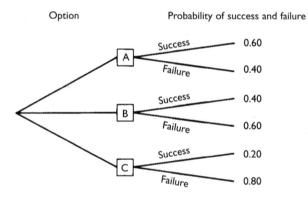

Figure 3.2   A decision tree

Linear programming

Linear programming is a mathematically based technique used to determine the best combination of limited resources which can achieve the desired objectives. It is especially useful when objectives can be measured and data quantified, for example when allocating tasks to machines when different tasks take different times and the machines have limits on the number of tasks they can complete in a period.

THE ADVANTAGES OF DECISION-MAKING TECHNIQUES

All the decision-making techniques detailed above try (in various ways) to attribute values or costs to different courses of action in order to provide some yardstick with which to judge possible plans against each other and against the objectives of the decision-maker. These techniques often take account of a project's risk or probability of losses. The use of decision analysis has the following advantages:

1 It focuses thinking on the critical elements of the decision.
2 It helps to structure problems and encourages organized thought.
3 It helps to uncover hidden assumptions behind a decision and clarifies its logical implications.
4 It simplifies the evaluation of alternative plans.
5 It helps to identify areas where more information is needed.
6 It provides a framework for planning contingency.

INFORMATION AND INFORMATION TECHNOLOGY

Any decisions made can only be as good as the information on which they were based. If managers receive incorrect, unclear information, or if they do not receive all the information that they need, then their decisions are liable to be poor ones. Overloading managers with information about a problem is almost as bad as not providing them with enough information. Too much data will often mean that significant information is overlooked – lost among the superfluous facts and figures.

To avoid this, the organization has to develop a good information processing system which provides its managers with relevant, timely and accurate information. This information should come both from the outside environment, and from inside the company (in the form of feedback and control reports).

Management information systems do not have to be IT based. However, microcomputer systems do allow managers to access all the information that they need instantly, and can allow them to work out the consequences of alternative solutions before making any decision, and thereby help them to avoid costly and irreversible errors of judgement. The importance of a logical information system which allows communication between components is crucial. In several large organizations, including the Health Service, there have been problems of systems not communicating and large quantities of data having to be reinput. The time and effort wasted carries a high cost. Some fund-holding general practices have gone as far as to computerize patient records to such an extent that computers assist in treatment (by identifying allergies, prior drug routines and effectiveness) and, in some cases, diagnosis.

Routine decisions dealing with routine problems can be programmed into a computer system. This will allow corrective measures to be taken quickly and easily (for example the automatic reordering of materials when items in stock fall to a certain level, thus helping to prevent expensive stock-outs), and will allow managers to concentrate on more important, non-routine decisions.

The extensive use of computers in stock control and manufacturing processes has made the application of 'Just In Time' procedures much 'cleaner' by virtue of a higher level of automation in stock levels maintenance and parts ordering.

SUMMARY

Decision-making is fundamental to the whole task of management, and is closely linked to the management processes of planning and problem-solving.

Most decisions, especially those taken by lower levels of management, are fairly routine ones, and are encountered many, many times. Some of these routine decisions can be programmed into computer systems. However, the decisions taken by senior managers are of a different nature. These involve choosing between different, often risky, strategies in order to solve ill-defined and unclear problems.

There are a variety of decision analysis techniques, and, together with a systematic approach to decision-making, they can help managers to make these second types of decisions, or at least to reduce the risk of making costly mistakes.

Good decisions are based on good information: an effective and efficient management information system should improve the quality of decisions at all levels of the organization.

CHECKLIST: CHAPTER 3

From this chapter you will have knowledge of:

1 Levels of decision-making:
   - Supervisors and junior managers see results of decisions
   - Higher management suffer a delay between the decision being made and its effects becoming clear
2 Theories of decision-making:
   - Classical theory
   - Behavioural theory
   - Satisficing
3 The decision-making process:
   - Define problem
   - Gather facts

- Develop alternative solutions
- Evaluate solutions
- Select the best
- Analyse the consequences
- Implement decision

4 The problem-solving process:
- Refer to Figure 3.1 for the steps in problem analysis and decision-making

5 Steps in decision-making:
- Statement of aims
- Examination of resources
- Look for alternatives
- Evaluate alternatives
- Select the best action
- Implement

6 Decision analysis techniques:
- Marginal or incremental costing
- DCF appraisal
- Cost–benefit analysis
- Sensitivity analysis
- Risk analysis
- Decision tree analysis
- Linear programming

7 Information and information technology

4 Organizing

Organizing is that part of the manager's task which involves coordinating and directing the company's resources in such a way that the company can carry out its objectives. Managers can control very substantial resources in terms of people, money, time, materials, equipment, etc., although it is the organization of the first of these, i.e. people, which takes up most of a manager's time and attention.

In this chapter we will look at some of the ways in which organizations coordinate and arrange the work of their employees to enable all the necessary tasks to be carried out effectively. Different organizational structures and reporting relationships will be examined, together with some principles of organization. The next two chapters will cover the more 'human' topics of how managers can motivate and lead or guide their subordinates and workforce. Here we will concentrate on the physical, organizational framework of the company.

THE TASK OF ORGANIZING

Urwick (1958) defined the purpose of organizing, from the view of an administrator:

> The purpose of organisation is to secure that this division [the separation and specialisation of tasks] works smoothly, that there is unity of effort or, in other words, co-ordination.

Much of the task of organizing involves establishing a framework or structure of roles for people in the organization to fill. This means that all the tasks which have to be done to allow the company to accomplish its objectives are assigned to people who are able to carry them out competently. Organizing, therefore, involves identifying the activities which need to be done to achieve these objectives; grouping these activities together into departments; assigning such groups of activities to managers; delegating to the managers the authority to carry the tasks out; and setting up a structure for coordinating all these activities, both horizontally and vertically within the organization.

PRINCIPLES OF ORGANIZATIONAL STRUCTURE

There are various elements (or principles) of organizational structure which tend to be common to most businesses. One set of these principles was published by Urwick in the 1940s (which he subsequently revised in the early 1950s). They provide a useful starting point for discussion, and so are listed here:

1 *The principle of the objective.* Every part of the organization must be an expression of the purpose of the undertaking concerned, or else it is meaningless and, therefore, redundant.

2 *The principle of specialization.* The activities of every member of any organized group should be confined, as far as possible, to the performance of a single function.

3 *The principle of coordination.* The purpose of organizing, as distinguished from the purpose of the undertaking, is to facilitate co-ordination and unity of effort.

4 *The principle of authority.* In every organized group supreme authority must rest somewhere. There should be a clear line of authority from the holder of supreme authority down to every individual in the group.

5 *The principle of responsibility.* Managers have absolute responsibility for the acts of their subordinates.

6 *The principle of definition.* The content of each position (the duties involved, the authority and responsibility it contains, and the relationships with other positions) should be clearly defined in writing and given to all concerned.

7 *The principle of correspondence.* In every position the degree of responsibility it carries and the authority it confers should correspond.

8 *The principle of the span of control.* No person should supervise more than five, or at the most six, direct subordinates whose work interlocks.

9 *The principle of balance.* It is essential that the various elements of the organization should be kept in balance.

10 *The principle of continuity.* Organizing is a continuous process, and in every undertaking specific provision should be made for it (Urwick, 1952).

Unity of objectives

The importance of all parts of the organization working towards common, planned goals has already been stressed many times. Increased competition, both from domestic and international companies, together with scarce resources, mean that no company can afford the luxury of having parts of it following their own whims and not contributing to the business's objectives. This is particularly true of labour-intensive organizations in the private sector, where human resources play such a key role. It is an established part of the induction programme for new staff of Nissan Motor Company to examine in some detail corporate objectives and the importance of these objectives to the individual member of staff.

People are more likely to pursue the organization's objectives, rather than their own personal interests, if these objectives are clearly defined and widely understood. (Unfortunately, in public sector organizations political considerations often lead to objectives being blurred or, worse, constantly changed, with all the consequences of loss of efficiency that this entails.)

Delegation

Delegation is at the heart of the management task of organizing, and it is the process by which managers are able to get things done through other people. Delegation involves determining what has to be achieved, assigning tasks to subordinates, conferring the authority necessary to do the work upon the subordinates, and exacting responsibility for the accomplishment of the work.

To be effective, delegation has to be carefully planned. The following points are very important:

1 The subordinate must be given enough authority to carry out the task.
2 Although authority can be delegated, responsibility cannot, and so a manager cannot escape responsibility for the activities of the subordinates through delegation. However, at the same time, subordinates have an absolute responsibility to their manager for their work, once they have accepted a task and the right to carry it out.
3 Since authority is the discretionary right to carry out an assignment, and responsibility is the obligation to accomplish the task, it follows that the authority should correspond with the responsibility. For example, if a manager gives a subordinate the authority to sell certain items, that subordinate cannot be held responsible for customer complaints caused by badly designed products or faulty manufacturing.
4 The duties which are to be delegated should be clearly specified, together with a target for their achievement or a timetable. Written delegations of authority are extremely helpful

both to the person who receives them and to the delegating manager. The manager will be able to see more easily any conflicts of interest or overlaps with other positions, and will also be able to identify more clearly those things for which the subordinate can and should be held responsible. Where delegation is non-specific, managers and subordinates alike are forced to feel their way and to define the authority delegated to them by trial and error. In this situation, unless they are familiar with top company policies and traditions, know the personality of their boss, and exercise sound judgement, they can be placed at a distinct and unfair disadvantage.

5 Delegated tasks should be within the capability and experience of the subordinate. If the task is too much for the subordinate, then the manager has not done the job well and has delegated badly. An adage which is often quoted is that managers get the subordinates that they deserve (and, conversely, subordinates get the managers that they deserve). A manager who delegates badly, or who does not develop subordinates to take responsibility and do their work well, will end up with subordinates who do their work badly and who cannot accept responsibility.

6 Review sessions should be held regularly, in order for the manager to monitor subordinates' performance and to offer constructive advice. It must be noted, however, that continual checking on subordinates to make sure that no mistakes are ever made will make true delegation impossible. People often learn best by the mistakes that they make, and so a subordinate must be allowed to make errors, and their cost must be put down as investment in that person's development.

The advantages of delegation

Whatever degree of discretion a manager eventually decides to give to her subordinates the general principle is clear – senior managers should concentrate their time and effort on the major issues facing the organization. Most senior managers are overworked. Delegating tasks to subordinates whenever possible is, therefore, good management and makes business sense. The work will then often be done more cheaply; junior managers' job satisfaction will be increased (as their superiors' should be, as they will be freed from tasks which are perhaps routine to them, but which still present a challenge to their subordinates); and senior managers will be able to use their time more effectively. Delegation will also help to develop junior managers for further promotion.

The span of control

The span of control is the number of subordinates reporting directly to one manager or supervisor. There have been many different numbers suggested as the maximum number that a manager should have reporting to her. Urwick's limit is five or six, if their work interlocks. If their work does not interlock, then one manager can supervise more subordinates. However, the highest theoretical figure put forward is eight or nine people only.

Determining the span of control

The appropriate span of control does depend on a variety of factors. These include the following:

1 Whether the subordinates are qualified and capable of making decisions without constantly having to refer upwards to the manager. If they are, the number reporting to the manager can be increased.
2 Whether the manager is prepared to delegate authority to subordinates: if not, then the number of subordinates reporting to the manager cannot be very many.
3 If an organization has a well-developed, tried and tested communication system that feeds information quickly to and from senior managers, each manager is able to control and coordinate a large number of subordinates.
4 In the same way, a manager can supervise more people if the organization has a well-defined planning function and an agreed set of objectives.
5 Some organizations, particularly those in the public sector, depend a great deal on personal contact to operate effectively. These types of organizations will inevitably have small spans of control and their structures will contain many levels of managers and coordinators.

The effect of different degrees of technical sophistication on spans of control was shown by Joan Woodward in a study of 100 manufacturing companies (Woodward, 1965). The median span of control of chief executives in firms using unit production processes was four; that in mass-production companies seven; and in process production firms ten. The number of people that the first-line supervisors controlled also varied greatly, depending on the production process used: the average number in unit production firms was 23; in mass-production/large-batch firms 49; and in process production companies 13.

The 'scalar' principle

The 'scalar' principle is the idea that there is a vertical line of seniority/command from the highest to the lowest level in an organization, down which authority and responsibility run through the organization, from top to bottom.

The more clear-cut this line of authority, the more effective will be the decision-making process, and the greater the organization's efficiency. A clear understanding of this scalar principle is necessary for the proper functioning of the organization. Subordinates must know who delegates authority down to them, and to whom matters beyond their own authority must be referred.

Unity of command

Unity of command is another basic management principle. The more complete an individual's reporting relationship to a single superior, the less conflict there should be in instructions, and the greater the feeling of personal responsibility for results. In larger organizations, however, it becomes more difficult to observe this 'unity of command'. Some organizational structures, moreover, deliberately flout this principle (for example, matrix structures, which we will look at a little later on). This does create some problems, but under certain circumstances these problems are outweighed by the advantages that these types of structure bring.

TYPES OF ORGANIZATIONAL STRUCTURE

Organizational structure can be defined as 'the established pattern of relationships among the parts of the organization'. There are two types of structure, which tend to exist side-by-side: a formal structure, and an informal structure.

The formal structure

This is the organizational structure, designed by the company's senior management, to achieve the objectives of the organization, and to promote efficiency and effectiveness. Thus the design of the formal organization is guided by the principles of unity of objective (which have already been noted) and of efficiency. The principle of efficiency states that a structure is efficient if it helps people to accomplish the company's objectives with the minimum of unforeseen consequences and costs, i.e. if it promotes good management.

The formal structure of an organization is made up of the network of organizational relationships, the pattern of grouping activities into departments, and the degree to which authority and responsibility are centralized in the organization.

It must be noted that there is nothing inherently inflexible about the formal structure of an organization. On the contrary, if managers are to be able to manage well, the company structure must provide an environment in which individuals can contribute to the company goals. There should always be room for individual talents, likes and capacities, even in the most formal of organizational structures.

The informal structure

Within every organization, alongside the formal organizational structure there exists an informal one. This is based on personal relationships between individuals and groups, and as such is much more dynamic and less easily definable than the more rigid, formal structure.

In many ways, these informal structures are more powerful than the formal organizational links, because they reflect the present, real-world situation within the company. If the two structures diverge seriously, it may become necessary to formalize at least some of the informal relationships; otherwise communication channels may break down and managers could lose their freedom of action.

DEPARTMENTATION

The grouping together of activities and individuals within the organization is known as 'departmentation' – or the process of dividing the business into logical, coordinated departments. The main forms of departmentation are as follows:

1 *By function.* In this form of departmentation, which is the most common one, activities are grouped around business functions such as production, marketing and finance. Occasionally, organizations also have departments set up around managerial functions such as planning and controlling. In the case of Abbey National plc, activities are split into large retailing functions with separate departments for planning and marketing. Functional departmentation has an important advantage in that it is a logical and time-proven method of organization. It is also the best way of making certain that the power and prestige of the enterprise's basic activities will be argued for by senior managers. Another advantage of functional departmentation is that it follows the principle of occupational specialization, and so encourages the efficient utilization of people. It must be noted, however, that the more numerous and specialized the various departments are, the more difficult the task of senior management becomes to coordinate and manage the business.

2 *By geographical area.* It is obviously useful to have geographically based departments whenever it is important to be close to the territory in which the organization wants to operate. For example, a company based in Britain may consider that its market is the whole of Western Europe. Rather than attempting to do everything from its head office, it may divide up the sales function (and later the production func-

tion), placing a separate operation in each country in which it sells. Many retail organizations such as W.H. Smith break operations down into small geographic areas, e.g. Northern England, and appoint a Regional Manager responsible for the outlets in the area.

3 *By product.* As organizations grow, so the range of products they offer grows. At first, all goods and services can be handled using common facilities, but there comes a time when the volume being dealt with is so large that advantages are to be gained by treating each product as a separate division (or even company). Product is an important basis for departmentation, because it helps the organization to make the best use of economies of scale and specialized knowledge, as well as individual skills.

4 *By customer.* This form of departmentation is particularly common in service businesses, where it is felt that different kinds of customers require different treatment. One example of this is in banking, where the big clearing banks make a distinction between their business customers and their personal customers. It is also particularly common in the food manufacturing industry, where companies differentiate between the small independent shop and the large multiple supermarket chain. Thus Derwent Valley Foods will manufacture own brand snacks for Tesco, etc., but also sell Phileas Fogg through as many outlets as possible.

5 *By process or equipment.* The grouping of activities about a particular process or type of equipment is often employed by manufacturing companies. A good example of departmentation by equipment is the existence of electronic data processing departments. The purpose of such departmentation is to achieve economies of scale, although it may also be required by the nature of the equipment involved.

6 *By time.* Organizing according to time-scales, for example day and night shifts, makes sense where round-the-clock production is necessary.

7 *By numbers.* This method of departmentation involves counting off a number of people who are to perform the same duties and putting them under a manager. The essential fact of this way of departmentation is not what these people do or where they work, but that the success of the undertaking depends only upon the number of people who are doing the work. In large manufacturing operations such as Thorn EMI Lighting, groups of workers are organized into cells.

Often, several different methods of departmentation will be used within one organization. For example, a company may have a basic functional structure, but the marketing department is further divided by geographical areas, and by customer type.

ORGANIZATIONAL RELATIONSHIPS

There are five main types of formal organizational relationship which can exist in businesses: line, staff, functional, committee and matrix relationships. All of these relationships often exist together in the same firm.

Line relationships

Line relationships describe the direct working relationships between the vertical levels of the company's structure, i.e. it is the authority that every manager exercises in respect of subordinates. This is the most common type of organizational and working relationship. It has the advantages that formal communication channels up and down the organization are clear, that authority and responsibility are agreed upon, and that instructions and information can flow up and down between the individuals concerned. Line authority is the central feature of the chain of command throughout any organization.

Staff relationships

The nature of staff relationships in an organization is an advisory one. The function of people working in a purely staff capacity (such as personnel, finance, IT and administration) is to investigate, research, and give advice to the company's line managers. It is very important to make this distinction between line and staff relationships. Both managers and their subordinates must know whether they are acting in a staff or line capacity. If they are acting in a staff capacity, their job is merely to advise their line colleagues, not to order or command. It is up to the line managers to make the decisions and issue instructions.

However, in many organizations this difference between the line and staff functions is not so clear-cut. In such companies you will often find staff manager specialists who also have line responsibility over their own subordinates. For example, in Figure 4.1 the personnel manager has a staff relationship to the managing director on personnel matters, but also has line responsibility over employees in the training, employment, recruitment and health and safety sections of the personnel department.

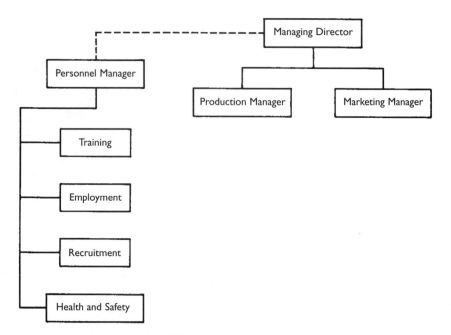

Figure 4.1   Line and staff relationships

Functional relationships

The third type of relationship operating within an organization is the functional relationship. Functional authority is the right which an individual or department may have to control specific processes or policies, throughout the company, because of the specialist knowledge or function. So, for example, a company's finance director will be responsible for the conduct of financial matters, but may also have the authority to make line managers follow and stick to the company's financial procedures and policies. It must be noted that functional authority is not restricted to managers of a particular type of department; it can be exercised by line or staff department managers.

Committee relationships

Committee relationships also play an important part in organizations. Committees can either be formal (i.e. have a written brief and the authority to carry out a specific task), or informal. Informal committees are usually set up for a particular, temporary purpose, for example to act as a pressure valve or as a sounding board for senior management.

Matrix relationships

Finally, there are what are known as matrix relationships. A matrix relationship is a combination of the other organizational relationships already discussed.

Matrix relationships involve subordinates and managers having dual responsi-bilities, first to their immediate superiors, and second to the specialist working groups of which they are members. Matrix structures can be set up for a limited period only – to see a particular project through, for example – or can be per-manent, normal parts of the organizational structure. British Telecom's research laboratories near Ipswich are organized on a matrix structure to allow staff to work together on particular projects while allowing divisionalization for other purposes.

Matrix relationships deliberately flout Urwick's unity of command prin-ciple, with people reporting to two authorities. However, the structure is the exception which proves the rule. The other main feature of matrix relationships is that they combine lateral and vertical lines of communication and authority (see Figure 4.2).

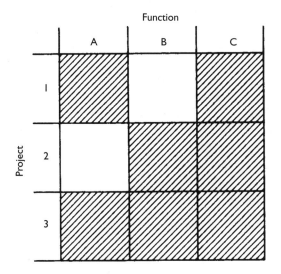

Figure 4.2 Matrix relationships

Matrix structures are very flexible, and can help an organization to adapt quickly to changes in its environment. They do have their disadvantages, however:

1 The allocation of resources and the division of authority between project groups and functional specialists can be a potential cause of conflict, and may lead to the dilution of functional management responsibilities throughout the organization.

2 There is also the possibility of divided loyalties on the part of members of project teams, in relation to their project managers and their functional superiors, because team members have to report to two bosses.

Despite these disadvantages, the matrix organizational structure probably offers the best answer to date to the problem of handling the tension between on the one hand the need to differentiate, and on the other the need to integrate, the complex activities of the modern organization. Any difficulties which do occur with such a relationship are probably best resolved in a less rigid organization, where most problems can be sorted out by informal, quick discussions.

CENTRALIZATION OR DECENTRALIZATION?

All organizations have to decide just what degree of centralized power and authority they will have in their structure. The inevitable push towards specialization in all but the smallest of businesses leads to the diffusion of authority and accountability. The need to structure activities leads logically to the need to allocate appropriate amounts of authority to those responsible for undertaking these activities. The senior management team of every organization of any size must, therefore, consider just how much authority to delegate from the centre.

The concept of centralization can be understood in a number of ways, for example in terms of performance and also in geographical terms. But when centralization is discussed as an aspect of management, it refers to the withholding or delegating of authority for decision-making. A highly centralized organization is one where little authority (especially over major areas of the business) is exercised outside a key group of senior managers. On the other hand, a highly decentralized company is one in which the authority to organize people, money and materials is widely delegated throughout every level of the organization.

The case for centralization

Centralization has a number of advantages:

1 Support services can be provided more cheaply on an overall basis, rather than on a departmental basis.
2 The company can often employ a higher calibre of staff.
3 Tight control can be kept over the company's cash flow and expenditure.

The case for decentralization

The advantages of decentralization are as follows:

1 It prevents the overloading of top managers by freeing them from many day-to-day operational decisions, and enables them to concentrate on their more important, strategic responsibilities.
2 It allows local management to be flexible in its approach to decisions in the light of local conditions, and thus to be more adaptable in situations of rapid change.

3 It speeds up operational decisions by allowing line managers to take immediate action, without referring back to their superiors all the time.

4 It focuses attention on to important cost and profit centres within the organization, and therefore sharpens management awareness of the importance of cost-effectiveness, as well as of revenue targets.

5 It contributes to staff motivation by enabling middle and junior managers to exercise real responsibility, and by generally encouraging initiative by all employees.

In reality, few organizations are either totally centralized or completely decentralized, but most are at least partially decentralized. This is mainly because of the enormous pressures on modern business organizations to delegate more and more authority to staff at executive and specialist levels. However, it should not be thought that this is a static principle: the amount of decentralization that occurs should vary as the circumstances of the company vary, in order to meet the needs of the situation at the time. For example, a merger between two companies might produce a greater degree of centralization for a while, especially if one company is experiencing financial trouble (often a catalyst for mergers). The quality of the organization's middle management will also determine the amount and pace of decentralization – if they are good, the senior managers are liable to delegate more and decentralize authority more. In many organizations (such as Ford (Europe)) the Treasury function is centralized to allow funds from various activities to be aggregated and invested in higher-yielding short-term investments.

ORGANIZATIONAL PROBLEMS FOR MANAGERS

Organizing the resources under their control is one of the most difficult of managers' tasks, and, whatever the solutions and structures ultimately chosen, most managers will encounter a number of problems. The first of these often arises out of imprecise, unachievable objectives which do not have the commitment of the employees concerned. Poor delegation and vagueness of working relationships also create problems for the manager, as well as lack of feedback, inadequate communication systems, and breakdowns in the chain of command, such as the mixing up of line and staff relationships.

SUMMARY

We have seen how organizing involves determining the physical framework or structure of the company in order to allow staff to work most effectively and efficiently.

The formal organizational structure consists of the grouping of activities into departments (based on area, function, customer, product, equipment, time-scale, or numbers); the organizational reporting relationships which exist in the company (line, staff, functional, committee and matrix); and the degree to which authority is centralized in the organization. Alongside the formal structure, there is usually an informal structure of personal relationships, which is just as important to the smooth running of the business.

To be most effective, the organization's structure should be as flexible as possible in order to adapt to changing circumstances.

CHECKLIST: CHAPTER 4

After reading this chapter you will be able to report on:

1 The organizing task:
   ■ Framework or structure of roles
   ■ Principles of structure
      – Express the purpose of the organization
      – Each group performs a single function
      – Clear lines of authority
      – Responsibility
      – Define content of each position
      – Responsibility should correspond with authority
      – Span of control should be limited to five or six
      – Keep in balance
      – A continuous process
2 Unity of objective – a common goal
3 Delegation – at the heart of the management task:
   ■ Give enough authority
   ■ Responsibility *cannot* be delegated
   ■ Authority should correspond to responsibility
   ■ Clearly specify duties
   ■ Within capability of subordinate
   ■ Review sessions
4 Span of control – determination of
5 Scalar principle
6 Unity of command:
   ■ Types of structure
      – Formal
      – Informal
7 Departmentation by:
   ■ Function
   ■ Geographical area
   ■ Product

- Customer
- Process
- Time
- Numbers

8 Organizational relationship:
  - Five main types:
    - Line
    - Staff
    - Functional
    - Committee
    - Matrix

9 Centralization or decentralization

5 Leading

In this chapter we will look at the management task of leading, or the directing and guiding of employees and subordinates to help them to attain the organization's objectives with the maximum application of their abilities. In the organizational context, a good leader can be regarded more as a good facilitator than as a traditional commander of people, although both types of leader benefit from a bit of charisma and the ability to inspire groups of people.

It must be noted that, although at times the terms 'leader' and 'manager' are treated as synonymous, there does need to be a distinction between leadership and management. *Leadership* is the ability to influence the attitudes and behaviour of others. *Management* is the formal process of decision and command. Leadership is one important aspect of a manager's job, but it is not all of it.

Here we will examine the importance of providing good leadership in companies, different theories about the nature of leadership, and the various styles of leadership which can be found in organizations, and their effectiveness.

THE IMPORTANCE OF LEADERSHIP

In his book, *The Practice of Management* (1955) Peter Drucker cautions against organizations relying upon leadership, instead of good management, because, although leadership is important, it is also very rare:

> Leadership is of utmost importance. Indeed there is no substitute for it ... but it cannot be taught or learned ... There is no substitute for leadership. But management cannot create leaders. It can only create the conditions under which potential leader-

ship qualities become effective; or it can stifle potential leadership. The supply of leadership is much too limited and unpredictable to be depended upon for the creation of the spirit the business enterprise needs to be productive and to hold together. Management must work on creating the spirit by other means. These means may be less effective and more pedestrian. But at least they are available and within management's control. In fact, to concentrate on leadership may only too easily lead management to do nothing at all about the spirit of the organization.

Certainly, however, leadership is an important element of effective management. The functions of management undertaken by the manager will produce far greater results if they have the ingredient of effective leadership added to them. When this effective leadership, or effective direction and guidance, permeates the whole enterprise, the result is a successful organization.

THEORIES OF LEADERSHIP

We will look at the three main leadership theories here: the personality or behavioural approach; the situational approach; and the contingency theory of leadership.

Personality or behavioural traits

The earliest studies of leadership were largely based on attempts to identify the personality traits that leaders possessed. In searching for measurable leadership traits, researchers took two approaches.

The first approach was to compare the personality traits of leaders and non-leaders. This was the most common approach, but it failed to identify any traits that consistently set leaders apart from their followers. As a group, leaders were found to be taller, brighter, more extrovert and self-confident than non-leaders. However, many people who are not leaders also possess these traits, while others who are acknowledged as brilliant leaders do not! For instance, two extremely charismatic, successful leaders – Napoleon and Alexander the Great – were both well below average height! The psychologist, E. E. Jennings, perhaps understood the real value of this approach when he wrote: 'Fifty years of study have failed to produce one personality trait or set of qualities that can be used to discriminate between leaders and non-leaders'.

The second approach was to compare the personality traits of effective leaders with those of ineffective leaders. This, too, has failed to isolate any traits which are strongly associated with successful leadership.

The situational approach

It was because of the inconclusiveness of the studies into the personality traits of leaders that the situational theory of leadership developed. According to this, people follow those leaders who they think are best placed to enable them to achieve their own personal goals and objectives.

The contingency approach to leadership

According to Fiedler (1967), people become leaders not only because of their personal attributes and personalities, but also because of the interaction between them and changing situations. Therefore, an effective leader is one who can adapt and lead in all situations.

Action centred leadership

John Adair further developed the contingency approach to leadership into the idea of action centred, or functional, leadership. According to Adair there are three variables in any work situation: task needs, group needs and individual needs. The effective leader has to be able to balance each set of needs against the demands of the total situation at that point in time. The leader has to judge which should have priority and at what time. This is a very flexible approach to leadership and depends entirely upon the circumstances of the situation.

Figure 5.1 shows how the three sets of needs are interconnected.

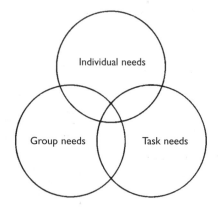

Figure 5.1   Action centred leadership

The interconnection of each set of needs means that action taken in relation to one particular set will have an effect upon the other two. For example, if the leader concentrates on building up group motivation, his action is liable to motivate the individuals making up the group as well, and the effect of both is usually to make the accomplishment of the task easier. Conversely, if the leader neglects one section of needs, the needs of the other two will not be met fully either – if task needs are ignored, then the group will cease to have goals to aim at and the individuals will have no occupation or purpose.

LEADERSHIP STYLES

Some earlier explanations of leadership styles classified them on the basis of how leaders use their authority. These regard managers as applying one of the three basic styles:

1 *Autocratic style.* The autocratic leader is seen as a person who commands and expects compliance, who is dogmatic and positive, and who leads and directs others by an ability to give or withhold rewards or punishment.

2 *Democratic/participative style.* The leader who uses this leadership style consults with his subordinates about proposed actions and decisions and encourages them to participate in these decisions.

3 *Independent/self-motivatory style.* This third style of leadership is one in which the leader gives subordinates a substantial degree of independence in their work, leaving them to set their own goals and discover their own ways of achieving them. The leader adopting this style sees his role as one of facilitating the activities of the others by providing them with information, and acting as a contact with the group's external environment.

McGregor's theory X and theory Y

The style adopted, whether autocratic or more participative, will depend in part upon the manager's view of human nature in general, and of the ability of subordinates in particular. McGregor (1960) set out two sets of contrasting views and assumptions about human behaviour: Theory X and Theory Y.

According to Theory X:

1 The average human being has an inherent dislike of work and will avoid it if possible.

2 Because of this human characteristic of dislike of work, most people must be coerced, controlled, directed [or] threatened with punishment to get them to put forth adequate effort towards the achievement of organizational objectives.

3 The average human being prefers to be directed, wishes to avoid responsibility, has relatively little ambition, [and] wants security above all.

Theory X managers will favour autocratic or perhaps paternalistic management styles.

In contrast, according to Theory Y:

1 The expenditure of physical and mental effort in work is as natural as play or rest. The average human being does not

inherently dislike work. Depending upon the controllable conditions, work may be a source of satisfaction or a source of punishment.

2 External control and the threat of punishment are not the only means for bringing about effort towards organizational objectives. People will exercise self-direction and self-control in the service of objectives to which they are committed.

3 Commitment to objectives is a [*result*] of the rewards associated with their achievement ...

4 The average human being learns, under proper conditions, not only to accept but to seek responsibility ...

5 The capacity to exercise a relatively high degree of imagination, ingenuity and creativity in the solution of organizational problems is widely, not narrowly, distributed in the population.

6 Under conditions of modern industrial life, the intellectual potentialities of the average human being are only partially utilized.

Theory Y thus encourages a more participative style of management, or at least consultative leadership, rather than leadership by the imposition of decisions.

Likert's styles of management leadership

Likert (1967) identified four styles of systems of management:

Style 1 Exploitative/authoritative
Style 2 Benevolent/authoritative
Style 3 Consultative
Style 4 Participative/group

1 *Exploitative–authoritative.* Managers who use this style of leadership are highly autocratic; they place little trust in subordinates and use fear and punishment as motivators, with only occasional rewards. They retain all powers of decision-making and only engage in downward communication.

2 *Benevolent/authoritative.* Managers using this style are paternalistic, placing a condescending trust and confidence in subordinates whom they motivate with rewards and some punishment. They allow some upward communication and opinions from their junior ranks and do also delegate some decision-making, although they retain close policy control.

3 *Consultative.* Managers using this leadership style seek out the opinions and ideas of subordinates and work to put

them to constructive use. They also engage in communication both upwards and downwards and encourage some participation in decision-making.

4 *Participative–group*. Managers who use this system show complete confidence and trust in their subordinates in all matters. They use the ideas and opinions of subordinates and motivate them through economic rewards and participation, and involve them in setting goals and undertaking appraisals of these goals. In effect, these managers operate as part of a group consisting of both peers and subordinates.

It is this *participative–group* style of leadership which Likert regarded as the most effective for managers. Its effectiveness comes from the group/unit concept that it operates upon. All the members of the group, including the manager or leader, adopt a supportive relationship in which they feel a genuine common interest in terms of needs, values, aspirations, goals and expectations.

> **INVESTIGATE**
>
> Which of Likert's styles of leadership do you think is nearest to that used in an organization you are familiar with, either in that organization as a whole or by your superior or supervisor? Do they differ at all? If so, how, and why?

The managerial grid – Blake and Mouton

Blake and Mouton's managerial grid (Figure 5.2) is a two-dimensional measurement of managers' leadership styles. One axis of the grid represents how production is valued, the other represents the human element in businesses – how people are valued. Scores are allocated from one to ten along both axes (1 = low, 10 = high).

Using this grid Blake and Mouton identified four extreme styles of management:

1 *Impoverished management*. This style of management is reflected in low scores on both axes as managers show little concern for either people or production values. They tend to be involved to a minimum in the requirements of management.

2 The antithesis of impoverished management occurs when managers are dedicated both to production values and people, scoring highly on both axes.

3 *Country club management*. Here the manager scores low on the production scale and has little concern for production

values. Instead, the manager is concerned primarily for people in the managerial role, and places great emphasis on promoting a relaxed and friendly environment. The creation of such a working environment is made at the expense of any coordinated effort to accomplish the organization's goals.

4 *Autocratic task managers.* These managers score highly on the production scale but low on the people scale. They are concerned only with developing an efficient operation and have little or no concern for people. They tend to be quite autocratic in their leadership style.

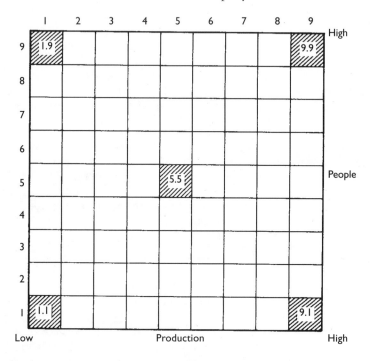

Figure 5.2   Blake and Mouton's managerial grid

EFFECTIVE LEADERSHIP

The thing to remember about all these different leadership styles is that they can *all* be effective, although at different times, and with different groups of people. Indeed, the best managers are those who do not use just one style all the time, but who recognize that during some situations they will have to exercise autocratic leadership, while during other circumstances they will be most effective by leaving people to work out their own goals and methods of operation.

Managers in charge of a group of research scientists would not be very effective as leaders if they used an autocratic management style, setting the group specific, daily targets to meet, and not consulting the group or listening to their opinions. Such a work situation clearly calls for a far more participative leadership style, where the manager acts as a group chairperson, facilitating the scientists' work.

On the other hand, if a hazardous chemical was released into the laboratory, the managers would not be showing particularly good leadership if they called the group together to debate what action they should take! In these circumstances, an autocratic leadership style is obviously required.

Reddin's three-dimensional theory of management effectiveness

The trouble with Blake and Mouton's managerial grid is that it is only a two-dimensional measurement of management style. It does not take into account that the four basic managerial styles can all be more-or-less effective, depending upon the particular circumstances in which the styles are used. As we have explained, the style that is most effective some of the time is not necessarily the most effective all of the time.

Therefore, to the two dimensions of Blake and Mouton's grid, Reddin (1970) has added a third, measuring 'managerial effectiveness' – or the extent to which the management style used meets the needs of the particular situation.

The Vroom–Yetton leadership model

Yetton and Vroom (1978) developed a model to show which of five management styles, ranging from autocratic to group decision-making, could be used effectively in dealing with different situations. Their work demonstrates that in practice managers do not usually just use one leadership approach or style, but do respond and adapt to circumstances (Yetton and Vroom, 1978):

> Whereas once there were only participative or autocratic managers, we now find that it makes as much sense to talk about participative and autocratic problems.

The five management styles are as follows:

A1   The manager solves the problem or makes a decision on the information available at the time.

A11 The manager gets any information needed from subordinates, and then makes a decision. The subordinates supply specific information in answer to the manager's requests; they do not define or discuss the problem at all.

C1   The manager asks the views of individual subordinates, and then makes a decision.

C11 The manager asks the views of subordinates in a group meeting, and then makes a decision.

G11 The manager shares the problem with subordinates as a group, and tries to reach a consensus decision. The manager's role here is really that of chairperson.

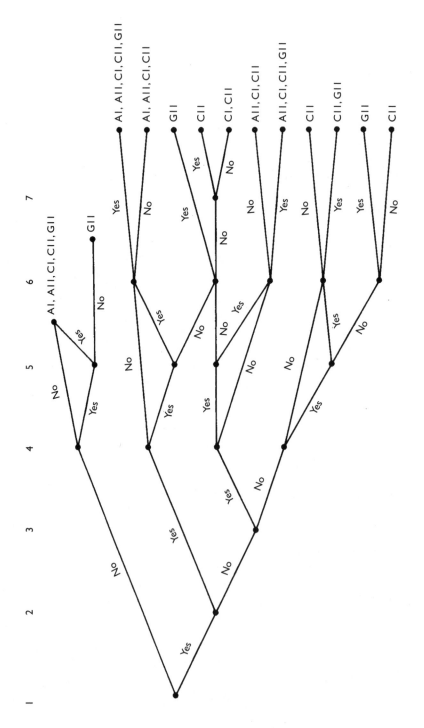

Figure 5.3   The Vroom–Yetton leadership model

Vroom and Yetton then define seven situational variables, in the form of questions, which should be used with the leadership model. These are as follows:

1 Does the problem possess a quality requirement?
2 Do I have sufficient information to make a high-quality decision?
3 Is the problem structured?
4 Is the acceptance of the decision by my subordinates important for its effective implementation?
5 If I were to make the decision by myself, am I reasonably certain that it would be accepted by my subordinates?
6 Do my subordinates share the organizational goals to be attained by solving this problem?
7 Is conflict among my subordinates likely with the preferred solution?

The leadership model, showing (in the form of a decision tree) the set of managerial styles which could be used in response to the questions/variables given, is illustrated in Figure 5.3.

SUMMARY

We have seen how leadership in a managerial context is about organizing, directing, guiding and helping people to do their work well.

There are several different leadership styles which managers may use to achieve this, ranging from an autocratic style, to a more participative approach as a facilitator. Each of these approaches will be effective in different situations: the mark of a good manager is knowing which style will be most effective in any given situation.

CHECKLIST: CHAPTER 5

After reading this chapter you will have knowledge of:

1 Theories of leadership:
- Personality
- Situational approach
- Contingency approach
- Action centred

2 Styles of leadership:
- Autocratic
- Democratic
- Independence of subordinates
- Likert's styles of management leadership:
  - Exploitative/authoritative
  - Benevolent/authoritative
  - Consultative
  - Participative
- Blake and Mouton's managerial grid
  - Impoverished
  - Enriched
  - Country club
  - Autocratic

3 Effective leadership:
- Reddin's 3D theory
- Vroom–Yetton model

6 Motivating

As well as leading and directing their staff, managers also have to motivate staff to work well in order to achieve the organization's objectives. In this chapter we will look at some of the problems that managers face in trying to motivate their staff, together with various motivation theories (from those concentrating on job content, to process and contingency theories), and some of the means that managers can use to motivate their workforce and subordinates.

WHAT IS MOTIVATION?

Motivation can be said to be the total propensity or level of desire of an individual to behave in a certain manner at a certain time. Within the context of the organization, motivation can be defined as the willingness of an individual to respond to the organization's requirements in the short run.

Everyone has what can be called latent energy, or motivation, within them which is *potentially* available. But this general state of being does not guarantee that an individual will behave appropriately in a given situation. The motivation within has to be directed towards a specific goal; it then becomes what is known as a 'motive for behaviour'.

Choices and priorities

Unfortunately, motivation is not quite so simple as that! It involves the person making choices from the available alternatives, about how best to allocate her energy and time. Most people are involved in many activities and groups, creating a multitude of relationships, and as the individual does not have unlimited time or energy, he must choose the activities on which to expend both. People tend to be more motivated in activities/relationships that offer the greatest perceived personal rewards or the fewest penalties, i.e. they will decide their own priorities.

It is important that managers understand this when they try to motivate employees, for from this it can be said that an individual who is not performing effectively within the organization is not necessarily lacking in motivation. Rather, the individual may not have been motivated in such a way as to give her role within the organization priority over other relationships and situations. Thus managers do not just have to motivate their subordinates; they have to motivate them in the right direction.

Motivation and personality

Motivation cannot be achieved in a vacuum independent of the individual's 'needs', 'wants' and 'fears'. Thus the central problem of motivation, as far as the manager is concerned, is how to induce a group of people with different needs, wants, fears and personalities to work together in order to achieve the organization's goals.

Needs and perceptions

The bases on which an individual's level of motivation is established are her needs and perceptions. Needs can be defined as desired, but as yet unrealized, goals; perceptions as organized impressions of her place in a particular environment, both as to the present and the anticipated future.

THEORIES OF MOTIVATION

Motivation theories can be divided into two types: content theories, and process theories. According to content motivation theories, which we will look at first, individuals are motivated by a 'package' of needs and wants which they pursue. Maslow's hierarchy of needs (1954), and Herzberg's two-factor motivation theory (1966) are examples of content theories.

In contrast, process theories of motivation examine the ways in which certain outcomes of events become attractive to people, and therefore are pursued by them. Process theories include Handy's motivation calculus, and Vroom's expectancy theory. Process theories differ from content theories in that they assume that individuals can choose their own needs and goals.

Management theories and motivation

The classical school of management theory assumes that workers are self-seeking, and only motivated by money, and so maximum productivity can be achieved by using assembly-line manufacturing processes with high rates of pay. However, breaking down tasks into their simplest elements, so that a day's work on (for example) a car assembly-line consists of repeating a task which has to be completed in under a minute several thousand times, creates mind-numbingly tedious jobs. Motivation will always be a problem in such industries, regardless of how much the employees are paid, and it tends to show itself in high staff-turnover rates, high absenteeism, and generally low morale.

The research of Elton Mayo in the early 1930s into productivity at the Western Electric Company showed conclusively that workers are not just motivated by economic motives, but that social contact and work-group self-government are also very powerful motivators.

Maslow's theory of human motivation

Abraham Maslow (1954) advanced a number of important propositions about human behaviour and motivation (Figure 6.1). First, he recognized that humans are wanting creatures, i.e. they want things, and continually want more. Even though specific needs can become satisfied, needs in general do not. Second, Maslow proposed that a satisfied need does not act as a motivator: only unsatisfied needs motivate behaviour. Third, human needs can be arranged in a series of levels – into a hierarchy of importance – consisting (in ascending order) of physiological needs, safety needs, social needs, esteem needs, and self-realization needs. As soon as needs on the lower levels of the pyramid are fulfilled, those on the next level will emerge as motivators and demand satisfaction:

Figure 6.1   Maslow's hierarchy of needs

> 1 *Physiological needs.* The lowest level needs are physiological ones. These are needs which must be satisfied to maintain life, and include the need for food, water, air, etc. Until these are satisfied they act as the primary motivators, taking precedence over any other needs. Thus a starving person

will not be motivated by desires for self-fulfilment, but by the need to obtain food.

2 *Safety needs*. The next level of the hierarchy is that of safety needs. These come into operation as effective motivators only after a person's physiological needs have been reasonably satisfied. These take the form of the desire for protection from physical danger, economic security, an orderly and predictable world, etc.

3 *Social needs*. The third level is that of social needs. Once again, these only become effective motivators as needs for safety become reasonably satisfied. They include the need to belong to a group, to be accepted, to give and receive friendship and affection. Social needs act as powerful motivators of human behaviour, but may be regarded as threats by an organization's management in some instances. For example, managers may regard some informal groupings within a company as threats to the company's operations and so seek to break them up.

4 *Esteem needs*. Esteem needs form the next level of the pyramid. These include both the need for self-esteem and for the esteem of others. Self-esteem includes aspects such as self-confidence, self-respect, knowledge, etc. The esteem of others includes the need for their respect, recognition, appreciation, and for status in others' eyes. The competitive desire to excel is an almost universal trait. This is a major esteem need, and if properly harnessed by management can produce extremely high organizational performance. A manager's stimulation of these needs can bring feelings of worth and value; if they are unfulfilled this can result in feelings of inferiority, helplessness and weakness. However, unlike the lower levels of needs, esteem needs are rarely completely satisfied, and tend to be insatiable.

5 *Self-realization needs*. At the pinnacle of Maslow's needs' hierarchy is the need for self-realization. This is the individual's need for realizing his own potential for self-fulfilment and continued self-development; for being creative in the broadest sense of the term. The specific form of these needs will obviously vary from one individual to another.

Money as a need

You may have noted that Maslow did not include pay or money as a need in his pyramid. He considered money as a means of satisfying various other needs at the different levels, but not as a specific need in itself. Money is of course more important in satisfying the lower levels of needs in the hierarchy.

Qualifications of Maslow's theory

Maslow's theory of needs can be applied generally, but not specifically. It is a dynamic picture rather than a static one. In addition, it must be recognized that levels in the hierarchy are not rigidly fixed, but do tend to overlap. Another problem with the theory is that the chain of causation may not always run from stimulus to individual needs to behaviour. Although the theory states that a person deprived of two needs will want the more basic of them, the person may not act so logically, as other factors may also be having an influence.

Further problems associated with Maslow's theory are that the same need will not lead to the same response in all individuals. Individuals may develop substitute goals if they cannot satisfy a particular need directly; and many of the things which humans strive for are remote, long-range goals that can be achieved only through a series of steps.

Herzberg's two-factor theory (1966)

Herzberg has provided an alternative explanation of the ways in which factors such as salary, achievement, and working conditions affect people's motivation to work. He asked 200 engineers and accountants about the factors which improved or reduced their job satisfaction. Two distinct groups of factors were identified:

Hygiene factors	Motivating factors
Company policy	Achievement
Salary	Recognition
Supervision	Responsibility
Working conditions	Job itself

Hygiene factors

Hygiene factors were those factors which created a favourable environment for motivating people and prevented job dissatisfaction. They included company policy and administration, managerial supervision, salary, interpersonal relations and working conditions. If any of these factors were felt to be substandard or poor, there tended to be job dissatisfaction. However, the presence of such hygiene factors did not in themselves create job satisfaction.

Motivating factors

Motivating factors promoted job satisfaction by their presence, but only when hygiene factors were also present in satisfactory levels. Motivating factors included achievement, recognition, the work itself, responsibility and advancement. The common element in these motivators is that they are all related to the intrinsic nature of the work itself; they are not merely elements or circumstances surrounding the job.

Herzberg's work shows that satisfaction and dissatisfaction are not simple opposites. Each is governed by its own group of factors: satisfaction by motivating factors and dissatisfaction by hygiene factors. To remove the causes of dissatisfaction is not the same as creating satisfaction.

If this is correct, it has important implications for managers in general, and personnel managers in particular. For example, the provision of welfare services may improve the working environment, but will not in itself motivate people to work.

Maslow and Herzberg

There is a strong similarity between Maslow's hierarchy of needs and Herzberg's classification of factors influencing motivation and job satisfaction or dissatisfaction. Herzberg's hygiene factors correspond to Maslow's physiological, safety, and social needs, whereas motivating factors correspond to the higher personal growth needs in the hierarchy.

Self-realization Esteem needs	Motivating factors
Social needs Safety needs Physiological needs	Hygiene factors

McClelland – motivating needs

David McClelland identified three basic motivating needs which, to some extent, correspond to Maslow's social, esteem and self-realization needs. McClelland measured the levels of these needs in various individuals, discovering that the existence of one need did not mean that the other two did not exist; rather, that an individual could be strongly motivated by a combination of all three needs.

McClelland's three motivating needs were as follows:

1 *The need for affiliation.* People with a strong need for affiliation usually gain pleasure from a group within which they enjoy intimacy, understanding and friendly interaction, and are concerned with maintaining good relationships.

2 *The need for power.* Those with a strong need for power want to exercise influence and control. They seek positions of leadership and influence, and tend to be argumentative, demanding, forceful, and good communicators.

3 *The need for achievement.* People with a strong need for achievement have an intense desire for success, and an equally intense fear of failure.

Further research by McClelland showed that, as a group, managers have strong needs for achievement and power, but low affiliation needs. Although those managers who have strong achievement needs tend to advance faster than others, it must be noted that to be a successful manager requires other characteristics besides a burning drive for success and achievement. Managers normally spend their days interacting with other people, and they have to work and get on well with others. Therefore, a need for affiliation is also important in managers.

PROCESS THEORIES OF MOTIVATION

Herzberg, Maslow and McClelland's theories of motivation are content theories. We will now look at some of the more recent process theories of motivation.

Equity theory – Adams

In his equity theory, Adams (1963) puts forward the idea that the absolute situation of workers is less important than people's situations *in comparison* to other similar workers, or to what these people feel their situations ought to be. Any perceived inequalities, for example in wage levels, tend to create unease and dissatisfaction, and will thus affect the individual's motivation to work. This dissatisfaction caused by perceived inequalities is often demonstrated by workers when they compare their pay scales and living standards to other similar workers, e.g. the UK car industry has been renowned for leapfrog pay claims between Vauxhall and Ford.

Two important points should be noted. First, that the situation of the person may not actually be unfair, but is just *perceived* to be unfair. Second, this unease will be caused even if the inequality works in the individual's favour, as well as if he thinks he is getting a bad deal. If people do not think that they are being adequately rewarded for the effort they put into a job, either by money or recognition, they will reduce that effort to a level which they think is appropriate for the rewards they receive.

Expectancy theory – Vroom

According to expectancy theory (1964), the level of motivation that an individual feels for doing a particular activity depends upon the extent to which the results are expected to contribute to her own particular needs and goals.

Following on from this theory of expectation, it can be said that the strength of an individual's motivation is a factor of the strength of preference for the particular outcome, and the expectation that this outcome will occur if certain behaviour is used or actions carried out. This is shown in Figure 6.2.

Normally, this calculation is not consciously made each time a person decides to do something. But certainly for major decisions, such as whether or not to change jobs, most people do at least weigh up the points for and against such a move.

$$M = P \times \left(\frac{Ex}{E}\right)$$

where M = strength of motivation
       P = strength of preference for outcome
       E = effort needed to secure outcome
       Ex = expectation outcome will occur

Figure 6.2   Motivation calculus

The contingency approach to motivation

Theorists such as Kurt Levin point out that an individual's motivation cannot be looked at in isolation because people interact with life outside the organization, and also with others inside it. So the motivation of a person depends upon more than just his needs and expectations, and will change according to circumstances. Being complex, even fickle creatures, different people react in different ways to things, and an individual's level of motivation can change from day to day and from hour to hour, depending upon how he feels. Figure 6.3 shows how an individual's level of motivation can change over a week.

WAYS OF MOTIVATING STAFF

Chris Argyris (1964) maintains that the work situation of an individual will affect the personal development and potential of that person. He identifies seven stages of development from infant to mature behaviour:

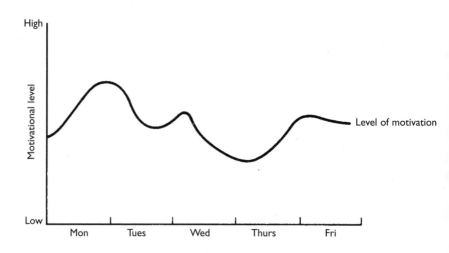

Figure 6.3   Changing levels of motivation

1 Infant passivity	$\rightarrow$	Adult activity
2 Dependence	$\rightarrow$	Independence
3 Limited behaviours	$\rightarrow$	Many different behaviours
4 Erratic and brief interests	$\rightarrow$	Stable deeper interests
5 Short time perspective	$\rightarrow$	Longer time perspective
6 Subordinate social position	$\rightarrow$	Equal/superior position
7 Lack of self-awareness	$\rightarrow$	Self-awareness and self-control

Argyris argues that many organizations still do not encourage their staff to develop mature patterns of behaviour in their work: jobs are reduced to minimal routine tasks, wider thinking is discouraged, and most staff take no part in making decisions. In other words, the organizations are promoting and encouraging McGregor's Theory X management. (This was discussed in the preceding chapter.)

In contrast, Argyris would like to see companies practising Theory Y management: encouraging greater participation by their employees, better communications, and job enlargement and enrichment, so that people have the opportunity to develop as individuals. This would benefit the organizations as well as their employees by removing many causes of dissatisfaction, as well as helping to motivate people more by allowing them more responsibility and respect.

Job enrichment, defined by Herzberg as 'the planned process of upgrading the responsibility, challenge, and content of the work', can definitely increase a person's motivation, as it tends to give the individual involved more power over decisions which affect him, and generally adds to the interest and responsibility of the job. (Although, of course, the extra responsibility of the work has to be rewarded appropriately.)

Job enlargement increases the number of operations performed by one person in one task cycle. This is more of a hygiene factor, removing dissatisfaction, because it should help to reduce the repetition and boredom of the work, although it is unlikely to increase motivation among the workforce.

Unfortunately, there is no easy answer to give to managers on how to motivate their staff. Organizations try to increase worker satisfaction with pay incentives and bonuses, giving individuals a say in decisions which affect them, and increasing the interest and responsibility of jobs. Different companies, and different departments, will all need to use different ways.

Perhaps the best advice is 'do as you would be done by'. Consider which factors motivate you in your work – job satisfaction through responsibility, interest and variety in your work, recognition of your abilities and effort – and bear in mind that these factors will also probably be motivators for most other people, regardless of their position in your organization.

SUMMARY

Motivating employees in an organization is difficult, but very important, as people who are motivated and satisfied with their jobs work harder and are more productive than those people who are not motivated by their work.

People are motivated by a combination of needs, wants, and fears. Individuals will be motivated by different things at different stages in their careers and lives, as personal priorities change.

Job satisfaction and job dissatisfaction are not opposite sides of the same coin: removing factors which cause dissatisfaction, such as poor working conditions, will not increase job satisfaction, which is influenced by motivating factors such as responsibility and achievement.

CHECKLIST: CHAPTER 6

This chapter has given you knowledge about:

1 What motivation is
2 Theories of motivation:
- Management theories and motivation
- Maslow's theory of hierarchical needs:
  - Physiological
  - Safety
  - Social
  - Esteem
  - Self-realization
- Herzberg's two-factor theory:
  - Hygiene factors
  - Motivating factors
- McClelland – motivating needs:
  - Affiliation
  - Power
  - Achievement
- Process theories of motivation:
  - Equity theory – Adams
  - Expectancy theory – Vroom
  - Contingency approach
3 Ways of motivating staff

7 Communicating

Communicating is a vital part of management. It links all the management processes together, and managers could not do their jobs without communicating.

Communicating can be defined as 'an attempt to achieve as complete and as accurate an understanding as possible between two or more people. It is an act characterized by a desire in one or more individuals to exchange information, ideas or feelings'. A more concise definition can be given as 'the process by which people attempt to share meaning via the transmission of symbolic messages'.

Communicating involves an exchange of ideas and information. This exchange takes place between the organization and the surrounding environment (here, communication can be seen as a way of connecting the organization with the outside world), and also inside the organization. Effective communications within a company are essential for the success of the organization.

In this chapter we will look at the links between communicating and the task of management, the communication process, communication channels in organizations, and the impact of IT on communication systems and on management.

MANAGING AND COMMUNICATING

Communicating is synonymous with managing: you cannot manage effectively without communicating. Managers spend their days communicating with other people: with subordinates, peers, superiors, customers, suppliers, and so on, by telephone, face-to-face meetings, electronic mail, written memos and reports, etc. One study by Rosemary Stewart of 160 managers over a four-week period found that on average they spent two-thirds of their working time with other people – attending meetings, giving and receiving information and instructions, discussing matters with colleagues. Most of their remaining time tended to be spent preparing and reading reports (Stewart, 1970)!

Communicating is also an integral part of the other elements of the management process.

Communicating and planning

We saw in Chapter 2 that planning is used to guide the organization towards its intended objectives and goals. Communicating information to managers is essential to the planning process. Without accurate information, managers cannot formulate relevant plans, and it is only through the communication process that plans are relayed down the organization to those subordinates and employees who have to implement the plans and meet the targets set out in them.

Communicating and organizing

Similarly, managers need to communicate in order to organize. Organizing is aimed at prescribing specific activities which are required to achieve the goals and objectives identified within corporate plans, and it is very dependent on effective communication. Communication is needed to provide managers with an understanding of the goals they are trying to implement. The entire purpose of the organizational structure is to create an effective communication system up and down the company's hierarchy.

Communicating, motivating and leading

In order to lead and motivate their staff, managers have to be able to communicate with them. Perhaps the aspect of communicating which is most important here is not the one normally associated with bosses and their employees, i.e. downward communication from the manager to subordinates, but rather, upward communication. Communicating is always a two-way process, and although the image of managers is normally one of initiating communications, with others listening and receiving information, managers in fact spend more time on the receiving end of communications. A good motivator and leader is one who listens to people.

Communicating and control

Control was mentioned in Chapter 2 when planning was discussed. It involves setting standards, monitoring performance and correcting deviations from these standards. Control depends upon feedback, which means accurate, timely and appropriate communication to the correct people. (The control process is discussed in the next chapter.)

Figure 7.1 is a model of the management process and summarizes the interrelationship between communicating and managing.

THE PURPOSE OF COMMUNICATING

To sum up the last section, there are a number of important reasons why good communications are vital for management. These include the following:

1 *Decision-making*. Management is concerned with decision-making, and the quality of those decisions depends to a large extent on the quality of the information communicated to the decision-makers.

2 *Organizing*. Communication is vital in starting the organizational processes. These processes are concerned with acquiring resources, developing them, and transferring finished goods and services to the customers. These all involve work teams and reporting relationships, and unless decisions are conveyed to and from the appropriate people, none of the organization's tasks can be accomplished.

3 *Influencing*. Communicating is all about persuading, informing, and educating. Therefore, its effect is to mould opinions.

4 *Activating*. Another purpose of communicating is to initiate action. Communication, in effect, acts as the regulating mechanism for beginning, continuing, and halting the company's business.

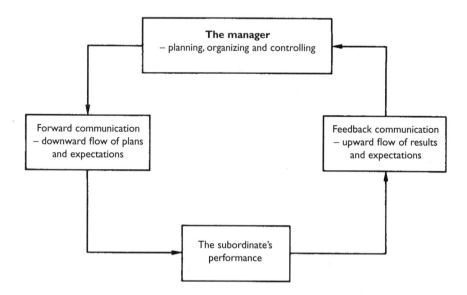

Figure 7.1   The management process

THE COMMUNICATION CYCLE

In order to use the resources at its disposal properly and effectively, management must carefully develop and maintain an adequate communication system. Certainly, one of the most basic skills that any management group must have is the ability to communicate.

The communication cycle (Figure 7.2) consists of five stages. All of these stages have to be completed for the process to be said to be a success:

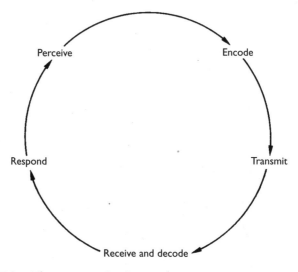

Figure 7.2   The communication cycle

1 *Perceive.* The communication process is centred around perception. This involves an individual assigning meaning to the signals he receives from the environment. The initiator of a message has received certain signals from the environment that he perceives as requiring attention. The purpose in communicating is to transmit information about initial perceptions to a second person. Therefore, the initiator must define clearly what he wishes to convey. If he is successful in structuring thoughts, the recipient of the message should in turn perceive the need for action. However, the perception of two individuals is never identical; rather, the communication is understood in similar ways by both parties through the use of common symbols.

2 *Encode.* Once the individual originating the communication has clearly perceived the need for action, and defined the thoughts he wishes to convey, he has to put these thoughts into a code using communication symbols that will be understood by the recipient. It is important that he expresses thoughts, intentions, and impressions by means

of symbols which accurately represent the message he wants to give to the recipient. These symbols can be written, verbal or any other symbols (such as expression, demeanour, etc.).

3 *Transmit.* Transmission is the sending of communication symbols from the message's originator to its receiver, either verbally or non-verbally. The selection of the method of transmission must be made after due consideration to cost, speed, accuracy, physical distance between the two parties, the need for 'personal' messages, and the type and quality of the transmission media available.

4 *Receive and decode.* Once the originator has sent out a message, the receiver must assign meaning to it. Thus the receiver must decode the message. This is essential, since the meaning that the message's receiver assigns to it governs the extent to which the communication process has been successful. If the receiver either does not or cannot understand what the sender of the message is trying to convey, then the process has not been successful.

5 *Response.* The final stage in the communication process is one of recycling. The receiver of the message considers the response he will make to the communication. This response will show just how well the original perception and message have been conveyed.

Data and information

It must be noted that, with regard to the human communication process, we have to differentiate between data and information. As far as human communication is concerned information can be defined as data which has meaning to the receiver. Data which does not convey meaning to the receiver is the equivalent of nonsense.

One purpose of communicating which has already been mentioned is to affect the behaviour of the message's receiver. It is therefore a mistake to assume that communication has been accomplished once the data has been transmitted. Transmission does not guarantee that the message's original intended meaning has been conveyed. Both the receiver and the person transmitting the message can affect the meaning ultimately communicated. The person sending the message has only limited control over what the person receiving it will perceive, while the receiver, because of a variety of reasons, such as personal background, psychological make-up, or 'noise' in the communication process, may see no meaning at all in the message, or assign to it a totally incorrect meaning.

HOW TO COMMUNICATE EFFECTIVELY IN ORGANIZATIONS

Although there are many possible standards that can be used to judge the effectiveness of a system of communication, speed, accuracy, and cost serve as representative measures. Businesses today need rapid and accurate communication and information systems. Decisions often have to be made at short notice because of the changing nature of the business environment. Nevertheless, these decisions must be based on adequate information. Therefore, an organization's communication system has to be capable of conveying large amounts of information quickly to and from the sources of the data and the decision-makers. At the same time, the system must be capable of transmitting accurate and timely information to the places at which it is required.

The principles of good communication

Effective communication is not solely a function of an effective communication system. We also need to look at the principles of, or criteria for, good communication, regardless of the system by which it is transmitted. The American Management Association (AMA) has suggested the following as principles of good communication:

1 The communicator must clarify ideas before attempting to communicate them.
2 The true purpose or message of each communication must be identified and examined.
3 The whole physical and human setting in which the communication is made must be considered carefully.
4 There needs to be consultation with other people when planning communications, so that conflicting or unintelligible messages are not sent.
5 The communicator should be aware of the overtones that are communicated in any message, as well as the message's basic content.
6 Every opportunity should be taken to convey something of help or value to the message's receiver.
7 Communications should be followed up in order to check that the intended meaning has been received and understood.
8 Communications need to be supported by the sender's actions, or else conflicting and contradictory messages will be transmitted to the receiver.
9 Good communications depend on a willingness to listen and understand, by both parties.

The following additional principles are also required for effective communications:

1 *Integrity*. Both personal integrity and integrity on the part of the organization. The integrity of the organization depends partly on supporting the position of middle- and junior-ranking managers. Since they occupy centres of communication networks, the organization should encourage them to use their positions for this purpose. Thus it is important that senior managers do not go over the heads of their subordinates and contact employees directly, unless it is unavoidable, because this risks undermining their subordinates' authority.

2 *Clarity*. The sender of a message is responsible for formulating the communication and expressing it in a clear and understandable way. If this is done, it should overcome some of the barriers to effective communication, such as badly expressed memos, faulty translations and transmissions, unclarified assumptions, bad handwriting, etc.

3 *Trust*. Trust is the key to effective interpersonal communications. Employees will not send accurate and open messages to their manager unless they trust the manager. They must have confidence that the manager will not use the information they have given her to the employees' detriment. They must believe that the information will not be inappropriately or inaccurately transmitted to other people, and that the information they give to the manager will be treated fairly on its own merits.

BARRIERS TO EFFECTIVE COMMUNICATION

We have seen how important communication is for coordinating activities within an organization, and for bringing about action. Because of this it is very important to understand what sort of barriers may prevent effective communication, and how these barriers might arise. These may be identified and explained as follows.

Lack of preparation

Inadequate preparation reduces the effectiveness of any communication. This failure usually arises from a belief that there already exists a ready-made package of information, which needs only to be directed towards the appropriate recipients to bring about the required effect. This is a mistake. Time and thought needs to be given to communicating. The person initiating the message needs to be clear about objectives; needs to consider alternatives; and then select the form of the message. A conscious choice of communication techniques must then be made. For example, would a notice of redundancy be best conveyed in person, or by telephone or letter? A curt letter of dismissal would inform someone adequately that they had lost their job, but the same message delivered in person would normally soften the blow.

Lack of clarity

Another problem with communicating lies in a tendency for messages to be vague and lack clarity. This often leads to costly errors and costly correction procedures.

Lack of openness

A lack of openness on the part of both the sender of the message and the receiver is a frequent cause of poor communication. The sender of the message should not give only part of the information needed. In the same way, the message's receiver must be prepared to listen to the information, and to accept it, even if it is unwelcome. This is especially important when the information is given by a subordinate. If managers only accept information that they want to hear, then eventually they will either only receive messages which are untrue, or receive no information at all.

Assumptions

Unclarified assumptions which underlie many messages also cause problems and prevent effective communications.

Premature evaluation

Rodgers, in *The Seven Point Plan* (1970), points to the tendency to jump to conclusions prematurely when receiving information, instead of keeping an open mind and judging the message objectively.

Differing cultures and backgrounds

The problems caused by different social backgrounds, different cultures (both organizational and social), age differences, jargon differences, and so on, which prevent clear communications between parties, should *never* be underestimated.

COMMUNICATION CHANNELS

Organizations have two basic kinds of communication channel within their structures: formal channels and informal ones.

Formal communication channels

Formal communication channels are those which are officially designed and recognized by the organization for the transmission of official messages inside or outside it. The formal channels are determined by the organization's structure and the organizational chart, detailing the official lines of authority, reporting relationships, and where responsibility and accountability lie. All these relationships involve communication. For instance, the exercising of authority can be seen as a downward flow of information from a manager to a subordinate. Communication through formal channels can be complicated, however, by the fact that subordinates do not communicate in the same way with their managers as they do with their peers.

Informal communication channels

An informal communication network (or 'grapevine') is essential for the successful operation of a company. A typical informal network involves members within the same level of the organization, and (depending on how formal or informal the general organizational structure and atmosphere are) can also involve employees at different levels of seniority. It cannot replace the formal communication channels, but it can complement and enhance them.

The formal channels are often static, while the organization they seek to activate is dynamic and must react quickly to changing situations. The informal network is more flexible and is able to convey information with amazing speed and accuracy. Thus the informal communication channels act as very beneficial, rapid problem-solvers in many companies.

Team briefings

The formal and informal communication channels tend to merge in team briefing groups. These groups are small (usually less than 30 people) and are arranged on a regulated but informal basis. The communicator is of a higher status than the rest of the group – either a supervisor or manager – and the purpose of the meetings is to inform the members of the group of what is happening within the organization, what is expected of them, and so on. This downward communication is important, but so is the informal feedback which results from this face-to-face contact and discussion.

Team briefings and discussions also help to improve employees' morale and commitment, as they are able to feel that they can make more of a personal contribution to the organization.

INFORMATION TECHNOLOGY AND COMMUNICATING

The IT revolution has had a significant impact on communications within organizations and on their managers. At a very minimum, the latest communications and computer technology enable businesses to deliver information and data far more quickly to the people who need it, and at a lower cost, than they ever could before. The latest technology in digital computers can transmit everything – voice, data, or image – by converting them into a stream of computer on–off pulses, and communication networks are now being updated to become multifunctional links carrying everything from telephone calls to television pictures. At the same time, new ways of sending digital information are dramatically lowering the cost of sending messages over vast distances.

The spread of powerful personal computers throughout businesses and organizations, together with an array of sophisticated software packages, means that managers at virtually all levels have access to accurate, highly detailed information and figures (for example, on sales levels of product X, broken down into regions).

This *should* lead to better planning and decision-making, and tighter control over variances from those plans. However, managers often become swamped with too much information – simply because of the availability of the detailed figures – and poor communication systems which do not provide managers with the information reports appropriate to their needs, position, and seniority. The detail in reports, like the plans that the reports give feedback on, should be inversely proportional to the seniority of the manager. Details of weekly sales and calls made by each sales representative in an area should be provided to the area sales manager, not to the company's sales and marketing director!

SUMMARY

We have seen how good management depends upon good communications, both communication systems (providing information through formal channels up and down the company), and personal communication between peers, subordinates and superiors.

Barriers preventing good communications include lack of clarity in messages; badly prepared and thought-out communications; the different backgrounds of people, leading to misunderstandings; a lack of openness to information and suggestions; and the assumption that once a message has been given, it has been understood and the communication process has been successful.

The information technology revolution has meant that managers can get up-to-the-minute data and information on a huge range of company activities. However, it has also meant that managers are often swamped by the sheer volume of data, and so there have to be effective communications systems in place to make sure that the data that managers receive is accurate, timely, and, above all, appropriate to their needs.

CHECKLIST: CHAPTER 7

This chapter has provided information about:

1 Managing and communicating:
- Communicating and planning
- Communicating and organizing
- Communicating, motivating and leading
- Communicating and control
2 The purpose of communicating
3 The communication cycle:
- Perceive
- Encode
- Transmit
- Receive and decode
- Response
- Data and information
4 How to communicate effectively in organizations:
- Principles of good communication
- Check out AMA list 1 to 9
5 Barriers to effective communication:
- Lack of preparation
- Lack of clarity
- Lack of openness
- Assumptions
- Premature evaluation
- Differing cultures and backgrounds
6 Communication channels:
- Formal
- Informal
- Team briefings
7 Information technology and communicating

8 Control

The management process of control was mentioned briefly when we looked at planning in Chapter 2. Control is the measurement and correction of subordinates' activities and the production processes, to ensure that the enterprise's objectives and plans are being carried out. Here we will discuss the control process; control and information systems; control techniques; and quality control.

THE CONTROL PROCESS

There are three steps in the basic control process: the setting of standards; measuring the results achieved against these standards; and correcting any deviations which might occur. The process is illustrated in Figure 8.1.

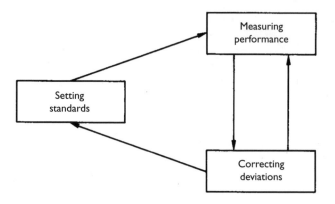

Figure 8.1   The control process

Setting standards

Effective control procedures are dependent upon good planning procedures. Without planning there can be no real understanding of the results which the organization is aiming for. The first logical step in the control process is, therefore, to draw up organizational objectives and plans. However, since company plans vary in both detail and complexity, and since managers cannot usually monitor everything, special control standards need to be established.

Standards are simply criteria of performance. They are points selected in the planning programme where performance measurements are made, so as to provide managers with indications of how things are going without having to check every step in the process.

The criteria of performance vary in nature. Among the best are verifiable goals or objectives, whether stated in quantitative or qualitative terms, which are regularly set in well-operated management by objective systems. As the best measures of the achievement of MBO plans are their end results, they provide excellent standards of control. These standards can also be stated in physical terms, such as quantities of goods produced, and so can easily be checked.

Measurement of results

The measurement of results actually achieved against the standards set should (ideally) be on a forward-looking basis, so that any deviations from the standards may be detected in advance of their happening, and avoided by appropriate remedial action.

If standards are appropriately set, appraisal of actual or expected performance is fairly easy. There are, however, many activities for which it is difficult to develop accurate standards, and many which are difficult to measure. If an item is mass-produced, then it may be simple to establish labour–hour standards and to measure performance against them. But if the item is custom-made, the appraisal of performance is often a far more difficult task; for example, Wedgwood have tussled with the problem of production of a plate as opposed to design. The first is easily quantified; the second has historically depended on the skills and requirements of an artist. Moreover, in the less technical kinds of work, not only may standards be hard to set, but appraisal may also be difficult. For example, measuring the performance of the senior finance manager, or the industrial relations director, is not easy because definite standards are very difficult to establish.

Nevertheless, as managers at all levels develop verifiable objectives, stated in either quantitative or qualitative terms, these aims become the standards against which all position performance in the organization's hierarchy can be measured.

Any accurate performance measurement has to depend heavily on the relevance, accuracy and timeliness of control information, or feedback. Such information comes from a variety of sources within the organization. The single most important source is the management accounting department, which is responsible for producing regular operating statements, expenditure analyses, profit forecasts, cash flow statements, and other relevant information. We will look at control information and techniques in more detail later.

Correcting any deviations

The manager's task of correcting any deviations which may occur between the standard results and the actual results is made easier if standards are set which reflect the organizational structure, and if performance is measured in these terms, since in this case he will then know exactly where, in the assignment of individual or group duties, the corrective measures must be applied.

Once the deviations have been identified and analysed, the manager must develop a programme for corrective action, and implement this in order to arrive at the results required. The development and the implementation of corrective programmes are likely to be time-consuming tasks. For example, in the case of quality control, it may take a considerable time to discover exactly what the cause of factory rejects is, and more time to put corrective measures into effect. This time-lag in the management control process shows how important future-directed control is, if control is to be effective. What managers need for an effective control process is a control system that tells them, in time to take corrective action, that problems will occur in the future if something is not changed now.

Control as part of the management task

The correction of deviations in results is the point at which control can be seen as part of the whole system of management, and where it is linked to the other processes in the management task. Managers can correct deviations by redrawing their plans or by modifying their goals, or by exercising their organizing function, through a reassignment or clarification of duties. They may also seek to correct deviations by recruiting additional staff, by better selection and training of subordinates, or by firing employees.

CONTROL INFORMATION SYSTEMS

Effective control depends upon the generation and supply of relevant information. The qualities of good control information are as follows:

1 *Accuracy*. Accurate control information is needed to direct the manager's attention to those matters actually requiring control action. If the information is inaccurate, then the manager is liable to make incorrect and inappropriate control decisions.

2 *Timeliness*. The timeliness of information is important, since it is of little consolation to the manager to know that, although the information was accurate, it was received too

late to make use of it! Timely information will avoid control delays and encourage prompt control action.

3 *Conciseness*. Management information systems can produce vast quantities of information, but the manager needs relevant information which highlights the exceptional items which require attention.

4 *Comprehensiveness*. The information presented needs to provide a complete picture of events in order to prevent inappropriate control decisions.

Management information systems

The provision of good quality information, thanks to IT innovations, and the great expansion in the use of microcomputers, has led to the development of management and control information systems. Management information systems (MIS) are essential for providing information for control purposes, as they allow access to greater databases and fast analysis of company results and possible future trends than was ever possible before.

One brief definition of an MIS is 'a system in which defined data are collected, processed and communicated to assist those responsible for the use of resources'. An MIS is a collection of functional information systems. Thus, within most organizations the most frequently used control systems are financial ones. This is because success is almost always measured in monetary terms.

Control reports

The purpose of control information systems is to produce control reports. The information contained within these should, firstly, have a purpose (and be relevant to that purpose), and, secondly, be tailored to meet the particular needs of the manager concerned. There should be a hierarchy of control reports, so that each manager in the organization has responsibility for the activities over which he or she has authority.

Control and feedback

The information generated by control systems is known as feedback. The actual results are recorded, and the information fed back to the managers responsible for achieving the target performance. Early feedback is essential for good control, especially where unexpected deviations have occurred.

To be effective, the system of feedback must be designed to provide quick, accurate reports of any serious deviations from the planned performance levels. The system must also supply reports to the correct organizational levels, and be phrased in the same terms as the original plan. In addition, the feedback must reflect the needs of the company. We can categorize feedback into the following two types:

1 *Positive feedback*. This type of feedback causes the system to repeat or to further intensify the particular condition being considered.
2 *Negative feedback*. This feedback causes the system to report and correct a trend by taking action in the opposite direction. A control system which uses negative feedback is often referred to as 'homeostatic' in character.

CONTROL TECHNIQUES

Although the fundamental nature and purpose of management control does not change, a variety of tools and techniques have been developed over the years to help managers in the control process. Some are quite basic, while others are more complex and sophisticated. Some measure the organization's financial soundness, while others are concerned with production efficiency. Still others deal with employee attitudes and perceptions. Although control techniques vary widely in their design and in what they measure, they all seek the same basic objective: to detect any variations from predetermined standards in order to enable managers to take the appropriate corrective action.

Budgetary control

A budget is simply a statement, usually expressed in financial terms, of the desired short-term performance of an organization in the pursuit of its objectives. Budgets form action plans for the company's immediate future, representing the operational and management sections of the corporate plan (see Chapter 2). Using budgetary control, the target standards are the desired performance outcomes. Information relating to actual performance is then collected systematically, and any variances between the two are identified.

A budgetary control system is built up from the following basic stages:

1 *Forecasts*. These are statements of probable sales, costs and other relevant financial and quantitative data.
2 *Sales budget*. The preparation of a sales budget is based on an analysis of past sales figures and a forecast of future sales levels in the light of a number of assumptions about market trends.
3 *Production budget*. This is prepared on the basis of the sales budget. It involves an assessment of the productive capacity of the organization in the light of the sales level estimates, and a consequential adjustment of either (or both) to ensure a reasonable balance between demand and potential supply. Production budgets will include output targets and cost estimates relating to labour and materials.
4 *Capital expenditure budget*. The capital expenditure budget specifically outlines proposed capital expenditure on plant,

machinery, equipment, etc. Capital expenditure budgets should usually be tied in with long-range planning, because capital investments in plant and equipment usually require a long period for their costs to be recovered from operations which create a great deal of inflexibility.

5 *Cash budget* (Table 8.1). This is a forecast of cash receipts and outgoings, against which actual cash receipts and payments are measured. This is perhaps the single most important control tool for an organization, as the availability of cash to meet obligations as they fall due is the first requirement of business existence.

Budgeted costs are calculated using a system of standard costing. Under this, costs of such things as materials, labour, production, etc., are worked out under set conditions. It is these standard costs which form the basis for the forecasted costs in budgets. Variance analysis is the process of examination and investigation of the factors which have caused any differences between the standard costs budgeted for and the actual costs incurred.

It has to be said that if budgetary controls are to work well, managers need to remember that they are designed only as tools, and not to replace managing! Moreover, they are tools for all managers, not just for the budget controller. It must also be noted that to be most effective, budget setting and administration have to receive the wholehearted support of top management.

Table 8.1   A cash budget

	Jan. (£)	Feb. (£)	Mar. (£)	Apr. (£)	May (£)	Jun. (£)
Receipts:						
Sales	8 000	8 000	10 000	11 000	14 000	14 000
Interest			500			500
Total receipts	8 000	8 000	10 500	11 000	14 000	14 500
Raw materials	3 000	3 000	5 000	6 000	7 000	7 000
Wages	1 000	1 000	1 500	1 500	2 000	2 000
Tax	5 000					
Dividends				1 000		
Capital outlay			2 000			
Total outgoings	9 000	4 000	8 500	8 500	9 000	9 000
Net cash inflow/outflow	(1 000)	4 000	2 000	2 500	5 000	5 500

Break-even analysis

Break-even analysis is a valuable and relatively simple technique for managerial planning and control. A break-even chart (see Figure 8.2) shows how different levels of product sales will affect the profits of the business. The chart produces a break-even point, which is the level of operations where income and costs are equal. Sales figures above the break-even point are profitable, whereas sales levels below the break-even point are not.

Certain assumptions have to be made when using break-even charts. Among these is the acceptance of a static, unchanging environment, when in fact the environment is more likely to be a dynamic one. There is also an implied assumption that the revenue–cost relationship is a linear one. Nor can the chart be used beyond the budget period of the firm. Despite these limitations, break-even charts do have a basic practical value – if only as a first approximation of the profitability of a project.

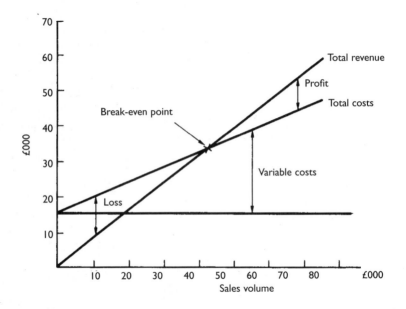

Figure 8.2   A break-even chart

Network analysis

The purpose of network analysis is to ensure that the shortest possible time elapses between a project's inception and completion, in order to keep delays and costs to an absolute minimum. To this end, a diagrammatic network of 'events' is drawn up in sequential order, with a time-scale for each part. The total time of the project is found by tracing the shortest way to the finish, i.e. by taking the 'critical path'.

The network of events can be extremely complicated, the critical path threading its way through a maze of different channels to find the shortest sequence of significant events. Such a highly complex network usually requires the use of a computer for the assessment, analysis, and scheduling of input data.

Whatever the type of network, the programme or project must be effectively controlled throughout the sequence of scheduled activities to ensure that its progress is as planned.

Network analysis has five important advantages as follows:

1 It forces managers to plan, because it is impossible to make a time–event analysis without planning and seeing how the pieces fit together.
2 It forces the whole company to coordinate its planning, because each manager down the chain of command must plan the event for which he or she is responsible.
3 It makes forward control possible.
4 It concentrates attention on the critical elements that may need correction.
5 The network system, with its subsystems, makes possible the aiming of reports and pressure for action at the right spot and level in the organization's structure, and at the right time.

Network analysis will not make the control process automatic, but it does establish an environment within the organization where sound control principles are used. It is also less expensive than might be thought in relation to other planning and control techniques.

THE REQUIREMENTS FOR ADEQUATE CONTROLS

If the control process is to be effective, it must meet certain requirements. These are as follows:

1 The controls should be tailored to the organizational positions using them. For example, what will do for a senior manager in charge of manufacturing will certainly not be appropriate for a shop-foreman.
2 Controls should reflect the structure of the organization. The more controls are designed to reflect the place in the organization where responsibility for action lies, the more they will enable corrective action to be taken as and when it is needed.
3 Controls should be tailored to the personalities of individual managers.
4 Controls should be flexible.
5 Controls should be objective.
6 Controls should be economical. Control techniques and approaches are most efficient when they detect and illuminate the causes of actual or potential deviations from organizational standards, with the minimum of costs incurred.

QUALITY CONTROL

The final aspect of control which we will consider is that of quality control. The assumption on which the control of quality rests is that in mass-production processes no two units are exactly identical. However, it is possible to mass-produce vast quantities of *almost* identical units. These units can be produced within certain tolerance levels, and a customer will accept variations between these tolerances, but not outside them. The role of quality control is to ensure that appropriate standards of quality are set and that variances beyond the tolerance levels are rejected. Quality control, therefore, is basically a system for setting quality standards, measuring performance against those standards, and taking appropriate action to deal with deviations outside the permitted tolerances.

Traditionally, quality control checking is very costly, and, since it represents an overhead in the production department, the amount of time and resources spent on it tends to be related to such factors as price, consistency, and safety and legal requirements.

One answer is for companies to start a programme of 'total quality control', such as has been part of many Japanese manufacturing companies for some time. Japanese firms, notably in the car industry, manage to instil a concern for extremely high quality throughout their production processes, and in all their employees. Each person on the shop-floor becomes personally responsible for checking and testing the quality of the goods that he or she makes, instead of using separate quality control inspectors. The aim, ultimately, is to achieve a level of zero defects in goods manufactured in their production process, making everything right the first time around. This means that the costs associated with rejecting goods and reworking parts which do not meet the given tolerance levels should be eliminated.

Of course, it is both costly and time-consuming to set up a system of total quality control. All the workforce have to be trained to check and inspect the parts and goods they make, and generally have to be trained to high standards of workmanship. Management also have to seek out and put right underlying causes of damage and reworking, instead of accepting wastage as unavoidable and inevitable, provided that it is kept below certain levels. However, firms that have set up such programmes have shown that in the longer term they allow the company to be extremely cost-effective and competitive, and that they can use the quality of their goods to a very effective marketing advantage.

SUMMARY

The process of control involves setting standards, measuring how far actual results meet those standards, and using this feedback to correct any deviations between the two.

Effective control is dependent upon accurate, concise, comprehensive and timely information in order to provide feedback reports.

Control techniques include break-even analysis,

network analysis, and (the most used of all) budgets, due to the fact that most standards tend to be expressed in monetary terms – being a common, understandable and measurable unit throughout any organization.

CHECKLIST: CHAPTER 8

This chapter has given you knowledge of:

1 The control process:
- Setting standards
- Measurement of results
- Correcting deviations
- As part of the management task
2 Control information systems:
- Accuracy
- Timeliness
- Conciseness
- Comprehensiveness
- Management information systems
- Control reports
- Control and feedback
3 Control techniques:
- Budgetary
- Break-even analysis
- Network analysis
4 Requirements for adequate control:
- Tailored
- Reflect structure
- Flexible
- Objective
- Economical
5 Quality control

9 Measuring performance

In order to achieve effective communication, motivation and control, it is necessary to have accurate performance measures in place. Historically, performance has been measured by financial criteria, but many companies have discovered the 'new' performance measures to be a vital part of any strategic management system: measures which are not only quantitative and financial in nature, and which are not geared solely to the maximization of future profits. Measuring performance by using information from existing management accounting systems has generated narrow measures which tend to look back and give a historical view of performance. There was a growing concern that these traditional models were failing.

WHY TRADITIONAL MODELS FAILED

As extensions to accounting systems, traditional performance measures produced information which was irrelevant to a strategic management initiative. The objectives of commercial strategy have changed from increasing throughput while keeping costs down to other fundamentals of product quality, timeliness and customer service. Traditional models provided information which was irrelevant and misleading, which would lead to poor decision-making, or at least would not contribute to good decision-making.

There were extended debates over the fundamental purpose of an organization, and for many years now the view that an organization exists merely to make money for its shareholders has been challenged. Rather, organizations may outline their function as meeting the needs of a number of different groups, which would include: customers; suppliers; and employees. The traditional way of providing financial measures required the processes within the organization to be interpreted financially so that performance measures could be applied. Delays and misinterpretation abounded!

In the past, individuals within an organization often viewed performance measures as a way of influencing behaviour, so that failure would be 'punished'. In reality, such a perception stifled innovation and experimentation, so that growth and development were difficult, if not impossible. Although this was not their intention, the perception of performance measures as 'big sticks' led to distrust and risk aversion which could devastate management strategies.

NEW APPROACHES AND MODELS FOR MEASURING PERFORMANCE

There are four approaches to measuring performance, which are in some respects interrelated. These are:

- Systems resource based
- Culture based
- Goal based
- Multi-actor based

The models that we will consider in relation to these approaches are:

- Total quality management (TQM)
- The performance pyramid
- Critical success factors (CSF)
- The balanced scorecard

Systems resource-based performance measures

Systems resource-based performance measures are based on the premise that the purpose of an organization is to survive, so performance measures focus on all key functions which contribute to the survival of the organization. In this type of measure the organization is a series of interactions with its environment. The criteria on which the performance measures are based are those which reflect the efficiency and effectiveness of the interface between the organization and the environment. Taking periodic measures provides a reading of the interface at that time, and a series of such 'snapshots' of performance in a changing environment enables remedial measures to be taken in between the snapshots.

Culture-based performance measures

Culture-based performance measures are closely associated with systems resource measures in that they relate to the factors which particularly distinguish the organization from others in its environment. The nurturing and improvement of its culture is what ensures the survival of the organization. The organization could be viewed as a living system of roles, norms and values which make up the specific culture – thus performance measures would include an assessment of the 'oneness' of the organization and the level of understanding between members.

TOTAL QUALITY MANAGEMENT

Total Quality Management (TQM) is a good example of these first two types of performance measure because TQM involves all members of the organization, and has been described as aiming to 'create constancy of purpose towards improvement of product and service with the aim of becoming competitive, stay in business and provide jobs' (Deming, 1986). Everyone within the organization is involved in TQM, which employs a comprehensive approach to the activity of the organization. TQM demands continuous improvement; thus there is a need to assess current performance for comparative analysis.

TQM performance measures should lead to the identification of best practice, which will contribute to organizational performance above that of competitors and beyond previous organizational achievement. The key point is the improvement of the process as a whole. Performance measurement in the TQM context can be considered in three main areas.

Customer focus

The TQM view of an organization is made up of customer–supplier chains. That is to say that the raw material supplier is a supplier selling to the raw materials purchase department (customer), who provides the manufacturing process with materials. The raw materials department is now a supplier to the manufacturing department (customer), and this continues through the entire process until the final customer. Figure 9.1 demonstrates the links.

Every process within the organization needs to be able to identify who is their supplier and to whom they themselves supply. The points of contact between supplier and customer at each stage are crucial. Opinions can be formed of product, process and organization on the basis of these short contacts. One measure could be an analysis of customer defections. Reicheld and Sasser (1990) argue that such an analysis would highlight problems with the service offered.

Process focus

In Figure 9.1, the 'manufacturing' circle may encompass the conversion of sand into glass and, whether the glass is for internal or external use, the process provides a visible link in the customer–supplier chain. To achieve optimal performance, each link of the chain must perform to the highest standard.

Control measures are used to determine whether the process is achieving the required standards; if achievement targets are not reached the process is stopped and remedial action is taken. This is determined by analysis of the performance measures which indicated the process should be stopped. The failure may be due to a common cause (i.e. part of the process) and can be rectified by controls, but special or extenuating causes can only be controlled by taking action which prevents them arising again. For example, if power fluctuation causes the process quality to vary, then the process itself is not at fault. Emergency alternative power supplies may well be sufficient to prevent the situation recurring.

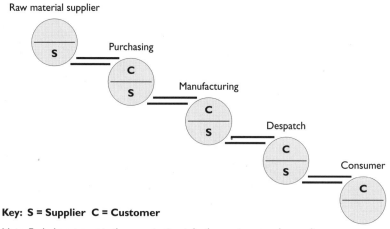

Key: S = Supplier C = Customer

Note: Each department in the organization is both a customer and a supplier.

Figure 9.1   Customer supplier chains

Improvement measures would be geared towards optimizing efficiency, effectiveness, productivity and quality, whilst minimizing waste. *Effectiveness* measures actual output against expected output and determines whether objectives are being achieved. While effectiveness measures concentrate on the outputs of a process, *efficiency* measures focus on inputs and compare resources used with resources planned to be used. *Productivity* measures the use of inputs in producing the required output and may be expressed as actual or expected (actual output/actual resource consumption; and expected output/expected resource consumption respectively). *Quality* measures are concentrated on the product or service and will reflect customer satisfaction. *Waste* is a measure of resources which did not add value to the product. An important measure in this instance is Cost of Quality (the aggregate cost of all activities to test, inspect and ensure the quality of the final product).

People focus

Owners and employees all have a role in the process of performance measurement. If the roles are optimized in the design and implementation of performance measures, then competent staff are motivated by the identification of best methods. TQM demands an ethos of innovation and continual improvement. Key areas of an organization which benefit from the TQM approach include:

1 High leverage process measures, which necessitate an intimate knowledge and understanding of the organizational process to be measured. The deeper the level of understanding, the more readily performance measures can be identified. Employees who work the processes on a day-to-day basis will bring a detailed insight to the measurement task, and definitions will ultimately be more useful and will lead to greater improvements.

2 There will be many employees within the organizational sectors (see Figure 9.1) who will never feel themselves to be in contact with customers. This may mean that they perceive their role as rather insignificant and unimportant in the process chain. If these same employees are concerned with the design of the TQM process then individual contributions to customer satisfaction cannot only be identified but measured also.

3 Employee input into the design of measurement systems means that measurements will be in a language readily understood by the workforce and timed in a way to be useful in remedial action.

4 An organization instituting performance measures may face a range of employee reactions. Often these reactions can include misgivings and doubt, leading to a fear of the system itself. This may largely be because of a lack of understanding of the system and its purpose. Involvement in the design stages of the system can only increase understanding and reduce fear, resulting in a greater likelihood that the system will be accepted when it is in place.

5 One of the consequences of misunderstanding is employees' desire to manipulate the system to produce results they think the managers want to see. This means that measurements may be skewed or distorted to produce an erroneous impression. Decision-making based on the information thus produced must be of dubious value. Thus employee involvement in design and implementation will improve the measurement system's usefulness. This is not, however, to say that industrial relations can be based on this sort of cooperation. TQM can be used as a supplement to existing worker/management relationships.

There have been suggestions that TQM systems themselves should be subject to performance measurements to determine their own effectiveness. Although this is a time-consuming process, Philip Ullah (1992) argued that it was worthwhile because it enables, for example, production of information on cause-and-effect relationships between the organization's reward system and employee attitudes to quality.

Goal-based performance measurement

Goal-based performance measurement is the third approach to performance measurement. This approach presupposes that the organizational purpose can be translated into organizational goals by management. Another assumption it makes is that the levels to which these goals are achieved can be used as an indication of the effectiveness of the organization. The goals-based approach requires the goals of the organization to be common throughout the organization, and for all levels within the organization to have accepted the goals as targets for performance achievement. Gregory and Jackson (1992) described such an organization as a 'well oiled goal achieving machine'. Comparison of results allows actual achievements to be measured against targets and provides the necessary information for remedial action.

THE PERFORMANCE PYRAMID

The performance pyramid is an example of goal-based and systems resource-based performance measurement systems. Adhering to TQM principles in the context of strategic goals and objectives, the performance pyramid gives a performance model which is both a top-down and a bottom-up (strategic and process) performance measure. The pyramid allows translation of management vision into performance indicators and operational measures. See Figure 9.2.

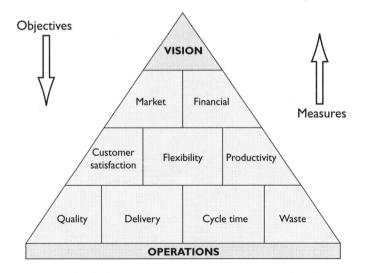

Source: *Measure Up! Yardsticks for Continuous Improvement*, R. L. Lynch and K. F. Cross, 1991, Blackwell.

Figure 9.2   The Performance Pyramid (1991)

The focus on strategy requires performance measurements to provide a continual comparison between estimated and actual gains in order to highlight necessary remedial action. New systems create their own enthusiasms which fade over time, but the system provides a climate of accountability and commitment to strategic goals which should be sustainable in the longer term. By providing information on the effect of adopted strategies and highlighting individuals' contributions to the achievement of strategic goals (thus informing and motivating individuals) the comparisons of actual to expected outcomes are achieved.

Performance measures of strategic goals are essentially in a context definable by market and financial objectives. Measures include market share, cash flow, profitability and market position. Objectives laid down are achieved by improving customer satisfaction, organizational flexibility and productivity. Thus there are three key measures: customer demands need to be managed and satisfied; changes in customer demands need to be identified and met efficiently; and productivity must be effective. As the pyramid diagram suggests, the entire organization is monitored in this model, as opposed to individual units or departments. In contrast to the strategic focus, the process focus needs operational measures, which in turn require identifiable business systems. Lynch and Cross (1991) define a Business Operating System (BOS) as 'all the activities required to deliver a product/service to the customer'.

The flow of work illustrated in Figure 9.3 is from left (Accept customer order) to right (Deliver to the customer) and crosses departmental boundaries (Customer contact/Order processing/Despatch/Information systems) without

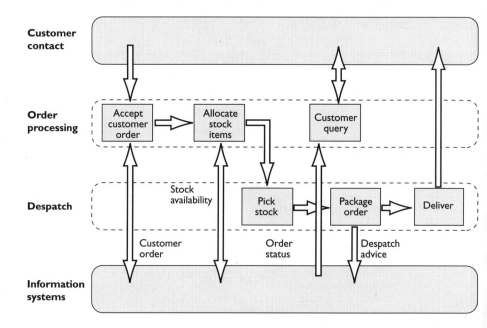

Figure 9.3   Business Operating System for simple order processing

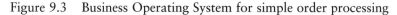

hindrance. The map indicates not only the customer/supplier relationships but also the cost drivers which affect the process as a whole. In terms of performance measures, there are two key identifications made here. The first is to demonstrate the individual's responsibility for establishing day-to-day operational control measures. The second, by highlighting the customer/supplier relationships, identifies activities which may usefully be measured. Measures would be geared towards maximizing quality and delivery whilst minimizing waste.

The balanced perspective of the diagram is achieved by the horizontal flow which reflects the cross-functional vision of the top level of the pyramid. The proponents of this type of model would argue that establishing measures at both operational and global levels makes a major contribution to the achievement of organizational goals.

THE CRITICAL SUCCESS FACTORS (CSF) METHOD

The performance pyramid is a combination of goals-based and systems resource-based models. However, there are approaches to measuring performance which are purely goal based. Of the two examined here, the first, the Critical Success Factors (CSF) method, is of the longest standing, being an early attempt at replacing cost accounting-based performance measures. The basic premise of the method is that concentration upon measures at a small level will increase the performance of the whole. Each area to be measured is known as a critical success factor, and can be measured at any level within an organization and will usually be unique to an organizational unit. Rockart (1981), a proponent of the CSF method, identified five main sources of CSF within an organization:

1 Organizations divided into industry sector will share CSFs that will be specific to that sector. For example, a factor affecting the automotive industry would be emission control standards, and all organizations within the industry would be required to meet standards, and common CSFs would be used to measure their performance against standards.

2 Some CSFs will be determined by the competitive strategy adopted by the organization. For example, if the strategy adopted is cost-led, then CSFs would necessarily include cost control and pricig policy.

3 Pressures from outside the organization in terms of the political, economic, social and technological environment may also influence the choice of CSF. For example, an industry using a labour force in short supply may well find industrial relations critical to survival and success.

4 Within an organization there are factors which have an influence for a short time only. While accepting that such factors do not constitute a long-term difficulty, measures are required to confirm that action taken is correcting the current situation.

5 Managers of units within the organization can be critical to the success of the whole organization. This means that managerial positions are critical success factors in two respects: first, at the level within the organization at which the manager functions; and second, in the activities in which the manager's unit is engaged. In addition, a significant influence on the performance measures can be the manager's understanding of what constitutes success or failure within the unit.

Having identified the CSFs, the next stage is to consider specific indicators for each CSF. Indicators will require the collection of information, both easily measured information and subjective assessments. There will tend to be a desire to use information that is easily collected – say from the accounting system. However, Rockart suggests that this is not a good source of information to use as the basis of the measures. It is clearly preferable for the measures themselves to drive the data collection process. This suggests a relatively high level of flexibility and change, given the list of CSFs above, which themselves are likely to change from time to time. Any measurement system must be able to respond quickly to any changes in the CSF. Flexibility is one of the key words and conditions for the success of the CSF method.

It should be noted that the basic premise that achieving low-level targets will lead to the high-level performance improving is not a universally held view, and has been subject to serious challenge. In fact, Blenkinsop and Burns (1992) and Harvey-Jones (1993) conclude that, rather than optimizing performance, managers become blinkered to opportunities for balancing performance across the chain of customer service. Difficulties occur in the simplification of the model to a point where it can no longer represent the real world and, even though relatively simple models are used, the implementation is complex and often requires specialist staff to oversee the process.

THE BALANCED SCORECARD METHOD

The second goal-based system is the Balanced Scorecard, which identifies success factors not within specific units or organizations, but applicable to all organizations. These have been termed 'generic success factors'. In this approach it is necessary to view organizations from a number of different perspectives. Kalan and Norton (1992) identify four key perspectives: Customer; Internal (i.e. activities key to the company's success); Innovation and learning (i.e. how to meet changing circumstances); Financial (i.e. investors' view of return on investment).

The aim of the organization's strategy is to identify goals and achieve objectives within each of these perspectives. Figure 9.4 illustrates some of the key goals and measures in each perspective and how they relate to one another.

The main thrust of this model is the balance between financial measures which are concerned with past performance, and operational measures geared towards future performance. Unlike other models, Kaplan and Norton insist that financial measures should not be ignored – in that a constant check must be kept to be sure that operational improvements are in fact contributing increased profitability. Undesirable effects on profitability would come about if manufacturing capacity was increased without an increase in sales. Financial measures, incorporated into the model, would check for this.

Measuring performance across all functions within the organization provides a comprehensive overall view which in turn should enable evaluations of the current strategy. Hazell and Morrow (1992) further suggest that this sort of model can be used in benchmarking best practice. This entails a comparison of one organization with another considered to be the best in the class. The information gained from the benchmarking process can then be fed back into the performance measurement process and may indicate new areas requiring measurement.

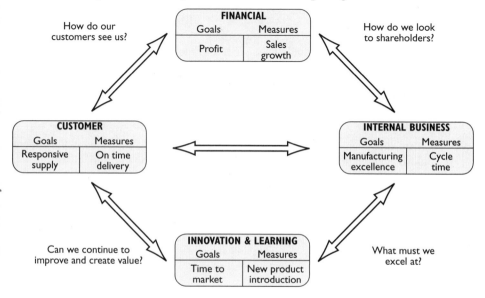

Figure 9.4   The Balanced Scorecard – Goals and measures
(from *Harvard Business Review*, Jan/Feb 1992)

MAKING IT WORK

Making a choice of performance measurement model depends on a number of factors. The models outlined above each use a variety of measures and are not clearly differentiated into type. The wide diversity of thought that has influenced the design of the models means that other factors have also to be considered in determining the most appropriate model for a specific organization.

Cultural fit

Managers and employees of an organization have some perception of the ethos of the organization in relation to measuring performance. Any system of measurement to be adopted must fit within that ethos or culture. Employees' mental image or model of what will or will not work also demands compliance from the performance measurement system. If such perceptions and models do not fit with the system, then there is a risk that information gathered for the system will be manipulated. Clearly, the models examined above vary greatly in their complexity. A very complex system will be less easily assimilated into existing mental models than a simple one.

Shared values

Organizations develop values which are shared and often prized. What has become the norm in an organization could be seriously upset by the application of an inappropriate performance measure system. For example, if a company has built a proud reputation upon teamwork and cross-functional sharing, then the introduction of a performance measuring system based upon departmental measuring – which often leads to a sense of inter-departmental competition – would be singularly inappropriate. Thus the measuring system needs to be sensitive to the existing employee/organizational structures.

Motivation

A performance measurement system, by identifying important functions within an organization, can contribute to motivation, especially when it is linked with a recognition and reward mechanism. Inappropriate or misdirected systems, however, can have the opposite effect and can even discourage desirable activities. In 1988, Pratt found that risk-taking and new ideas tended to be undermined by measurement systems which were bureaucratic and complicated.

In summary, the appropriate performance measurement system will take account of three key points:

- Are the concepts contained within the system relevant to those who will operate the system?
- Does the proposed system function well within the culture of the organization?
- If the current system engenders desirable features in the organization, what will happen to the desirable features when the new system is introduced?

The discussion of performance measurement systems has divided them into three main categories: goal-based; systems resource-based; and culture-based. The likelihood is that an organization will need a combination of types of performance measurement system. The more complex the organization, the more likely it is that a combination will be required.

Multi-actor-based performance measures

There is a fourth type of measure known as the multi-actor-based approach. This system assumes that the basic function of the organization is to satisfy the needs of stakeholders. Stakeholder satisfaction is determined by their interpretation of events within the organization and is largely externally focused, i.e. not within the operational scope of the organization. Measures are used to determine the level to which stakeholder expectations have been fulfilled. This type of approach, like the culture-based approaches, requires a higher level of expertise than goal-based and system resource-based approaches.

Other difficulties may occur after the choice of system has been made. Some difficulties will relate to the measurements to be taken and others to the diagnosis of the situation based on the information provided by the system. There are many functions which are easy to measure: products, results, physical objects. Measuring the system itself is not so straightforward. Goal-based and systems resource-based performance measures tend to focus on the easier to measure facets of a system. However, the diagnosis based on these factors is problematic because the measures have concentrated on the symptoms of the situation rather than identifying the problem itself. Thus diagnostic skill levels need to be relatively high if these two types of performance measure are to be used effectively.

Culture-based and multi-actor systems measure other factors, such as: staff attitudes; the system itself; leadership style; motivation, etc. In these cases the measurement system can be seen as being part of the organization itself, rather than an exterior system. As such, much greater skills are required at the measuring stage than with goal- and system resource-based models. Proponents argue that the information gathered for diagnosis is much more accurate and better targeted. The down side is that the more complex the approach, the less easily the system can be incorporated into the manager/employee mental models of what works. Figures 9.5 and 9.6 show the difference in structure between the relatively simple measures carried out by an 'outside' measurement system, and the more complex but more integrated approach of a system 'inside' the organizational system itself.

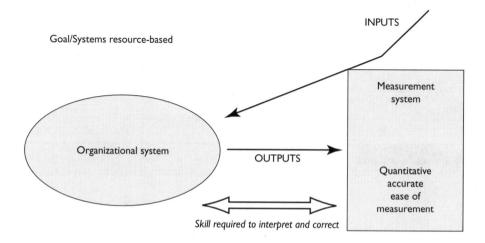

Figure 9.5   Measurement of the results of an organizational system

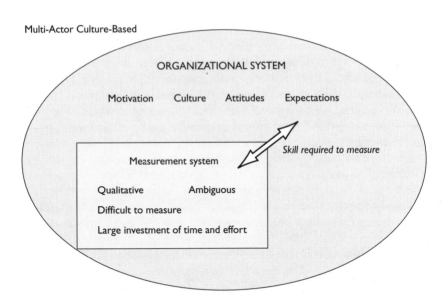

Multi-Actor Culture-Based

ORGANIZATIONAL SYSTEM

Motivation   Culture   Attitudes   Expectations

Skill required to measure

Measurement system

Qualitative   Ambiguous

Difficult to measure

Large investment of time and effort

Figure 9.6   Measurement of integral attributes of an organizational system

In order for a performance measurement system to be effective and efficient it must be relevant and coherent. Whatever the measurement system is, it must fit comfortably within the culture of the organization and must draw upon a number of approaches to create the best fit. In addition, the levels of skill and the resources that the performance measurement system requires must not be beyond those available to the organization.

INVESTIGATE

Outline the three main types of performance measuring model. Which elements of these models can you see in your organization? How is performance measuring data gathered in your organization, and by whom?

SUMMARY

This chapter has reviewed the areas in which traditional performance measures have failed to supply management with the information they need. We then considered some new models and how they might achieve levels of information that decision-makers look for. Finally, some new models of performance measure were outlined, and we discussed how they should be chosen and implemented.

CHECKLIST: CHAPTER 9

1 There are three main types of performance measure:
- Goal based
- System resource based
- Culture based

2 There are three factors to consider in choosing a performance measure:
- Relevance to management and employees
- Consistency with culture
- The effect on existing plus points in the organization

3 Performance measuring systems:
- Total Quality Management
- Performance pyramid
- Critical success factors
- Balanced scorecard

4 Implementation problems:
- Does the system fit?
- Will the staff accept it?
- Difficulties in taking measurements
- Difficulties in making diagnosis

Part Three
Management
Functions

10 Managers and departmental functions

Any organization has several common departmental functions, which, although they may not all have such clear labels, are the means by which the organization gets its work done. The functions of production, marketing, finance and personnel can be detected in all organizations which exist to provide goods or services to others, regardless of whether they are businesses or not.

These departmental functions are easily recognized in any company which manufactures goods to sell to others, but they are also present in service industries and in other organizations. Take a college or university, for example: here the production function is obvious – the lectures and courses it holds for its customers – its students. It has to market these courses in order to attract a new intake of students each year; while the finance and personnel functions are also obvious in such an organization. These functions are less clear, but still exist, in a very different organization, such as a church. Here, the 'production' function can be seen in the provision of church services and facilities for the local community, while the 'marketing' function can be recognized in the out-reach work of many churches to those people outside the church.

Managers in any organization will be concerned with one or more of these departmental functions at some point in their careers, although there are also other, more specialized, departmental functions in some businesses (e.g.

computer and data processing departments). As this is a book about the management task in general, this is not the place to consider any specific industry functions; but we can put the management processes we have just looked at in Part Two into the context of organizational functions.

PRODUCTION

The production department is of vital importance, as without the making or provision of whatever goods or services the organization has decided to specialize in, the organization has no reason to exist, nor (equally important) will it be able to generate the means to exist by selling such goods and services to customers. The production manager's duties include making sure that adequate levels of raw materials are stocked, and that there are appropriately trained and supervised people available in sufficient numbers to work together to produce the finished product. The manager also has to ensure that the organization's quality standards and scrap rates are adhered to, and that the goods are produced within budget.

MARKETING

Marketing is a great deal more than just selling – although selling is an important part of the function. Marketing involves finding out just what products are wanted or needed by consumers, and so helps to tailor production to meet those needs. It involves raising customer awareness of the company's products through advertising and creating 'brand awareness' and brand loyalty, through a combination of product quality and pricing strategy. In some organizations the marketing function also has responsibility for distribution – making sure that the correct goods are despatched to the correct retail or wholesale outlets.

The marketing function is vital for every company. There is no point in an organization supplying high-quality, reasonably priced goods or services which customers do not want or cannot be persuaded to buy. The Sinclair C5 provides a good example of a product which, when aimed at the wrong market, did not sell. Originally intended as a serious alternative means of transport for city commuters, the C5 eventually found its market niche, in America, as a fun runabout for children.

FINANCE

The finance function is responsible not only for controlling costs, paying salaries and creditors, and ensuring that sales invoices are paid by customers, but also for setting and monitoring the organization's annual budgets, longer-term capital expenditure plans, and borrowing levels. The finance manager is also responsible for dealing with the money that the company receives: making sure that profit targets and other earnings ratios are met, and investing spare cash in the money markets.

PERSONNEL

The personnel department has the job of recruiting new staff and training them so that the skills of the workforce meet the requirements of the organization. Training and developing a person's skills should be an on-going process throughout their career with the organization, and not just at the start of it. The personnel manager is responsible also for staff–management relations, grievance and disciplinary matters, and redundancy and dismissal procedures. The manager also has to ensure that the organization adheres to the equal opportunities and equal pay legislation, and does not discriminate against individuals because of their race or sex, or on the grounds of disability.

CHECKLIST: CHAPTER 10

After reading this chapter you will be able to identify the functions of:

1 Production
2 Marketing
3 Finance
4 Personnel

Part Four
The Managerial
Environment

11 The business environment

The manager's task has to be looked at in context. Both the organization and the work of its managers will be affected by the business environment in which they exist. This business environment has two forms: the external environment (common to all organizations); and the company's internal environment, or culture, which is unique to each organization.

In this chapter we will look at the internal and external business environments of organizations, and will then briefly discuss the management of environmental and business change.

THE EXTERNAL BUSINESS ENVIRONMENT

The external business environment in which organizations operate has a continuous and profound effect on their management. The different parts of this environment act both as constraints on business operations, and will present organizations with new opportunities to exploit. The way in which different organizations respond to these common constraints and opportunities determines which organizations are successful and which fail.

However, because organizations are open systems, importing resources from the environment (such as raw materials, finance, employees, etc.), and because organizations' activities are often subject to 'rights' or claims of interest groups in the environment, it is sometimes difficult to determine where the organization ends and the external environment begins. Therefore, the boundaries between the two are blurred. The company's employees are simultaneously involved in, and are a part of, the environment outside the company.

The boundaries between the organization and the environment are not static either. They are based upon relationships, rather than physical entities. Thus while certain fixed elements, such as its location, do have some impact on an organization's limits, it is the decisions of managers that really determine where the organization ends and the external environment begins. It can be said that different employees and their tasks are at the company's boundaries, depending on the activity at the time: sometimes it is the switchboard operator, while at other times it is the managing director.

Elements of the external environment

The external environment is made up of a number of different elements: the economic environment, the technological environment, the political and legal environment, and the social or cultural environment (see Figure 11.1).

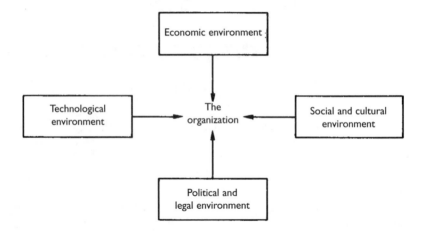

Figure 11.1   The external environment

The economic environment

The economic environment affects the organization because of two reasons. First, it relates to the effect of changes in the level of prices on the company; and second, the level of general economic activity in the country indicates the likelihood of consumer incomes rising or falling. This in turn will affect company sales, costs and wage rates.

The parts of the economic environment

The economic environment is made up of several parts, which all have a greater or lesser influence on organizations and business:

1 *The supplier*. The supplier provides the organization with raw materials and the other components it needs. The organization has to purchase these at a price (and quality) which it can afford, while at the same time it still has to make a profit from selling the finished goods.

2 *Customers*. Customers form another part of the economic environment, and affect the organization in that their needs and demands determine what a company produces and sells successfully in the way of goods and services, and the prices at which they can be sold.

3 *The investor*. Business confidence and the willingness of banks and other investors to lend money to companies are closely linked to expectations about the future level of economic activity in the country. Thus, the state of the general economic environment determines the ability of businesses to borrow money for capital investment purposes.

4 *The government*. The government is a particularly important element in the economic environment. Government fiscal and monetary policies influence the organization in relation to the cost and availability of credit, the level of taxation, interest rates, exchange rates (if the company exports its goods) and general business confidence.

5 *Competitors*. A company's competitors are simply a 'threat' in the economic environment. Thus, for example, any advertising promotion of Peugeot would have an impact on the sales of Rover.

The legal and political environment

The legal environment is a very important external constraint on organizations. The law sets out the operating conditions of most businesses, ranging from specific bans on certain kinds of behaviour, to regulations requiring the reporting of income and staffing at various times of the year.

Companies have to comply with laws setting minimum health and safety standards; laws on employment practices; laws banning discrimination on grounds of race, religion, sex, and marital status; trade union laws; and a whole host of other regulations specific to individual industries and businesses. Again, car manufacture provides a useful example, where Saab were using as part of their 1993 advertising programme the fact that they already comply with California car emission controls for 1994. With the introduction of improved technology, Saab continued to promote the environmental benefits of their products in the second half of 1996.

However, the legal environment has to be considered alongside the political environment, because it is the political environment that is responsible for bringing about the enactment of new laws and regulations.

The political environment consists of the government and parliament in the UK, together with the Commission, Council and Parliament of the EU. These bodies pass the many, many laws and regulations which affect the way organizations function. The network of laws, regulations, directives and court decisions presents a highly complex environment in which all companies and organizations must operate. The way in which an organization responds to this environment may well determine its success or failure.

An organization can respond to these constraints by studying prospective rules and legislation, in order to develop a business strategy which will deal with the new legal framework within the necessary time-span. For example, car manufacturers who have developed engines with the capacity to run on both leaded and lead-free petrol, before leaded petrol has been either totally banned or priced out of the market in favour of unleaded fuel, have neutralized this potential threat to their business.

You should note, however, that there are political influences on organizations and their managers regardless of any legal obligations. For instance, strong political pressure brought by conservation groups concerned about potential pollution risks have affected industrial companies (such as chemical manufacturers) independently of any legal ramifications.

The political environment is closely linked with the social environment. Laws are often passed as the result of social pressure on the government. The ability of political parties to make laws also depends upon popular acceptance of their social and economic ideas and policies at the polls at election time.

The social or cultural environment

The social or cultural environment is the third major element of the external business environment. It is made up of the attitudes, customs, beliefs, education, etc., of people and society at large. The most important determining factors of this social environment are the class, culture, age, sex and political beliefs of the people in it. The social environment has a significant influence upon organizations and the ways in which they are managed, because the organizations themselves are made up of people who are part of this external environment. An example of the social environment influencing business behaviour is found in W.H. Smith deciding to restrict selling publications likely to be viewed as degrading.

Closely linked with the social environment is what may be termed the 'ethical environment'. This consists of a set of well-established rules of personal and organizational behaviour and values. The ethical environment of organizations refers to justice, respect for the law and a moral code. The conduct of any company will be measured against these ethical standards by the company's customers, suppliers and the general public. The problem with 'moral ethics', however, is that the organization's view of the world may not always be in accordance with society's normal codes of morality! A number of unit trusts have been set up as 'ethical trusts' investing in companies who have equal opportunities policies, and no links with the armaments industry, etc.

The technological environment

The final element of the external environment is the technological environment. Recent developments in technology have had an enormous influence on the ways in which companies operate. Computers have revolutionized product design and manufacture; for example, the introduction of sophisticated automated or robotic machinery in the car manufacturing industry can now enable a group of people to do what required a mini-organization to do even just a few years ago. It has also changed work patterns away from the assembly line and back to the 'gang' or 'work group'.

Volvo in Sweden experimented with allocating teams to the construction of individual vehicles. Advances in technology have also made it possible to open up new markets which were previously unexploited, either because the technical 'know-how' was lacking, or because the costs involved were prohibitive. Offshore oil and gas exploration is just one example of this.

Technical developments and innovations can present enormous opportunities for companies. But there is a down-side risk attached to this. The rapid pace of technological change does mean that, unless businesses are careful, they can find their products and manufacturing processes becoming obsolete very quickly. Therefore, it is vital for organizations to pay a lot of attention to monitoring the technological environment and to try and forecast possible medium- to long-term changes in it.

THE TYPES OF ENVIRONMENT

The different elements in the external business environment tend to relate to each other in different ways, bringing about a particular set of circumstances which the organization has to react to. Emery and Trist (1965) called this the 'causal texture' of the environment.

Environments are considered to be made up of various 'good' and 'bad' elements, which have an effect upon the organization. Emery and Trist identified four types of environmental causal texture, each of which affect the organization and its management in very different ways:

> 1 *The placid randomized environment.* An environment in which the good and bad elements are relatively unchanging in themselves and are distributed randomly. In such an environment the organization need hardly plan strategically at all, and is able to act purely on a tactical basis.
> 2 *The placid clustered environment.* An environment in which the good and bad elements are not randomly distributed, but relate to each other and are grouped together in certain patterns. An organization must respond to this kind of environment with strategic, long-term planning, rather than merely short-term tactics. The tobacco industry often finds social, political and economic factors combining together.

3 *The disturbed reactive environment.* In this type of environment there is more than one organization of the same kind; indeed, the dominant characteristic of this type of environment is that several similar organizations exist together. In this environment each organization does not simply have to take account of the other competing organizations when they interreact at random; it also has to consider that whatever information it has may also be known by its competitors. Examples here include supermarket chains, where the policies of Sainsbury have an impact on Tesco, etc.

4 *The turbulent environment.* In this environment, dynamic processes, which create significant variances for the organizations which exist within it, arise from the environment itself. The organization operating in this type of environment thus faces a large degree of uncertainty, with the consequences of any actions becoming increasingly unpredictable. Markets which are subject to taste variations such as popular music suffer from this type of environment.

THE INTERNAL BUSINESS ENVIRONMENT

The internal environment, or culture, of an organization is made up of the unique combination of values, beliefs, behavioural patterns, and so on, which characterize the manner in which groups and individual employees of that organization work together in order to achieve their objectives. The individuality of businesses is thus expressed in terms of their differing cultures.

Four major types of organizational culture have been identified by Charles Handy (1984): the power culture; the role culture; the task culture; and the person culture.

The power culture

In this business culture power rests with a central figure of authority who exercises control through the selection of key individuals. An organization with this kind of culture operates with few written rules, and decisions are often taken according to the balance of influence at the time, rather than in accordance with logic or procedure.

The main strength of organizations with power cultures is that they are able to move and react quickly to any threat. However, whether the company does move quickly – or in the right direction – depends upon the person or persons in control. The success of organizations with power cultures therefore largely depends upon the quality of the individuals in control: the power culture puts a tremendous amount of faith in the individual. Such a culture is often found in new companies controlled by their entrepreneurial founders.

Size and growth do pose problems for organizations with power cultures. Often, successful businesses with this culture and dynamic founders grow comparatively quickly, and often rapidly become too big to be manageable by one person. If such a company is to remain a cohesive, controllable entity, it should really either create other subordinate organizations or develop a modified power culture whereby some standard management procedures are introduced to complement the existing control structure. Otherwise, such organizations risk becoming victims of their own success.

The role culture

The organization based upon the role culture is structured according to functions or expertise, for example the finance department, the personnel department, etc. Each of these departments is strong in its own right, but is coordinated by a small group of senior managers by means of set written rules and procedures, such as:

> Procedures for tasks/roles (i.e. job descriptions).
> Procedures for communications.
> Rules for settling disputes.

It is these rules and procedures which are the major source of influence in a role culture. This type of culture is perhaps better known as 'bureaucracy'.

In the role culture the role (or job) is the factor which is important; the individual is a secondary consideration. People are selected in order to perform a particular job and that job is usually described in such a way that a variety of individuals could do it. The organization's efficiency therefore depends not so much on the quality of individual people inside that organization – as in the power culture – but on the rationality of the allocation of work and responsibility.

The success of a role culture organization depends upon a stable environment. It will then provide security and predictability in terms of the acquisition and promotion of specialist expertise without risks. The drawback of role culture organizations is that they tend to be slow to perceive any need for change, and are slow to change even if that need is recognized. Organizations based upon the role culture tend to be found where economies of scale are more important than flexibility, or where technical expertise and depth of specialization are more important than product innovation or product cost.

The task culture

In contrast with the role culture, where the emphasis is on *how* something is done, rather than what is done, the task culture emphasizes the accomplishment of the task or project. In order to do this a task culture organization seeks to bring together appropriately qualified personnel in a team, and gives them the resources they need to do their jobs. The task culture provides team members with a substantial amount of control over their work, and employees also enjoy mutual respect within the group, based upon capability rather than age or rank. This culture harnesses the unity of the work team, with its goal of completing a particular project, in order to improve efficiency, and to identify the individual with the objectives of the organization as a whole.

Managers have the power to allocate projects, people and resources, and so they maintain control in the task culture. However, this is not control on a day-to-day basis; team members retain substantial control over their work, and indeed any attempt by senior managers to exercise closer everyday control would not be acceptable in this type of culture.

It is when there is a scarcity of resources that management often feels a need to interfere in the control of the project teams' work. Team leaders also start to vie for what resources are available, and, consequently, the task culture begins to change to a power culture.

The task culture is very adaptable and is, therefore, appropriate where flexibility and sensitivity to the market or to the external environment are important (i.e. where the market is competitive and the product life is short). Conversely, the culture is not suitable in situations which require economies of scale or great depths of expertise.

The task culture is popular with managers. According to Handy it is:

> the culture most in tune with current ideologies of change and adaptation, individual freedom and low status differentials.

Even so, it is not always the most appropriate culture for the prevailing climate and technology.

The person culture

In the person culture the purpose of the organization's existence is to serve the individual. The individual is therefore the central point in this culture. Organizations based upon the person culture are rare – usually they are family firms. Instead, one tends to find within another culture a person whose behaviour and attitudes reveal a preference for the person culture. A popular example of this is the person culture-oriented professor working within a role culture. The professor does what is necessary under the contract, teaching when required, in order to retain a position in the organization. Essentially, however, he looks upon the university or college as a base on which to build personal career and interests. These may, indirectly, add interest and value to the organization, although that would not be the professor's main motive for pursuing them.

Factors influencing organizations' cultures

The culture of an organization is a matter of its own choice. There are a number of factors which will help determine this choice, such as the following:

1 *Size*. This is a very important variable influencing an organization's choice of culture. The larger an organization, the greater the tendency towards formalization and the devel-

opment of specialized coordinated groups. Therefore, a growth in size generally influences an organization towards a role culture.

2 *Technology*. In general, routine programmable operations are more suitable to a role culture than to any of the other cultures, as are high-cost technologies which require close monitoring and supervision and depth of expertise, and technologies where economies of scale are available. However, power or task cultures are more suitable where organizations are involved in unit production and non-continuous operations. These latter two cultures are also more suitable when technology is changing rapidly.

3 *History and ownership*. Where there is centralized ownership of organizations, i.e. in family firms, there is a tendency towards a power culture. Diffused ownership allows diffused influence, based upon alternative sources of power.

4 *Goals and objectives*. Quality objectives can usually be monitored more easily in role cultures, while growth objectives are usually more appropriate in power or task cultures.

5 *The people*. The availability of suitably qualified people is a significant factor in any choice of culture. The individual preferences of key people in the organization will also have a large say in determining the dominant culture, irrespective of what it actually should be for the good of the company!

6 *The environment*. The final important factor influencing the choice of culture is the external environment. An unstable, changing environment requires an adaptable, responsive culture, i.e. a task culture, whereas a more stable environment may lead an organization more towards a role culture.

Differentiation

An organization might have a structure which reflects a single culture. On the other hand, different structures reflecting different cultures might exist side-by-side in separate departments of the same organization. This is known as 'differentiation', and should help the organization to adapt to changes in its external environment better and more quickly than it perhaps would if it had just one organizational culture.

However, to be successful, differentiation has to be both coordinated and integrated, or else there is a danger that the organization's staff will not work together towards any common aim or goal.

INVESTIGATE

What sort of culture does your company, college, or an organization with which you are familiar have? And what degree of differentiation, if any?

THE MANAGEMENT OF CHANGE

The ability of organizations to manage change effectively has become more and more important recently because of the rapid advances in technology and the increasing uncertainty and risk associated with the business environment. Companies which want to survive and prosper are having to be very much more receptive to new ideas and practices, and very much more responsive and adaptable.

In order to manage change, the organization must be properly prepared for it, from the top management team downwards. (This is often the sticking point – a board of directors or a chief executive who are isolated from what is really happening in the company by layers of management.) A climate of change can really only be successful if it has the overt backing of the senior executive. This is why change is usually easier to accomplish in task or power cultures, rather than in role cultures.

Managing change requires flexibility, a good planning and decision-making system, and an efficient management information system. Throughout this book I have tried to emphasize how often a contingency approach to management, to leadership, to motivation, and so on, is one of the more flexible and adaptable ways of managing people – the idea that what is the right answer in some circumstances is not necessarily the right answer in others. This approach also promotes an openness to different ideas and concepts. Systematic planning and information systems also help by enabling the manager to take decisions in the confidence that uncertainty and risk have been accounted for and minimized as much as is possible.

The possibility of change tends to provoke resistance among the people it will affect, due to a very natural fear and mistrust of the unknown. This resistance will show itself in different ways, ranging from an outright refusal to cooperate to a covert undermining of the proposals. (It should be noted that these reactions can be found all through the organization, from senior managers to workshop employees.)

This mistrust and resistance have been found to be best overcome by a deliberate policy of keeping people informed of what is being proposed, and getting them involved, as far as possible, in the discussions and decision-making. If someone has been able to suggest a new way of doing a task, or has at least been asked his opinion, he will be far more likely to be willing to give the solution a fair trial than if it has just been imposed upon him. However, these discussions should be genuine ones, and not held merely for form's sake, with no account taken of what is said by the people taking part.

SUMMARY

We have seen how the organization is affected by its external environment because, as an open system, it interacts with it, taking inputs from the environment and returning goods and people out into it again.

The external environment consists of economic, technological, legal and political, and social or ethical elements. These elements present both opportunities and threats to businesses, and combine to form different environment types: placid randomized; placid clustered; disturbed reactive; and turbulent.

There are four types of internal organizational culture: the power culture; the role culture; the task culture; and the person culture. Organizational culture choice is influenced by the organization's size; previous ownership; the technology it uses; its objectives; the environment type it operates in; and the people in it. Often an organization may have more than one culture in its structure at the same time – this is called differentiation.

The management of change has become more and more important, and is best achieved through a flexible and open system of management.

CHECKLIST: CHAPTER 11

This chapter allows you to identify:

1 Business environment:
   - External
   - Economic
   - Legal and political
   - Social or cultural
   - Technological
2 Types of environment:
   - Placid randomized
   - Placid clustered
   - Disturbed reactive
   - Turbulent
3 Internal business environment:
   - Power culture
   - Role culture
   - Task culture
   - Person culture
   - Factors influencing organizations' cultures
     - Size
     - Technology
     - History and ownership
     - Goods and objectives
     - People
     - Environment
   - Differentiation
4 The management of change

Part Five
Conclusions

12 Summary and conclusions

Over the preceding chapters we have looked at the management task from several angles. We have put the manager's task into its historical context, seeing how different management theories evolved and how they still influence current practices. We have seen how all organizations, regardless of whether they are profit-making or non-profit-making organizations, manufacturing companies or providers of professional services, have certain core departmental functions in common. The majority of managers will, at some point of their careers, be involved in one or another of these functions – production, marketing, finance or personnel – to some degree.

However, this is a non-function-specific book because, as we have discussed, there are certain key characteristics of the management task which apply to each and every management job.

'Management' is about planning on both short- and long-term bases; it is about making considered and judged decisions; it is about organizing the necessary resources (in terms of raw materials, machinery and people) in order to carry out the organization's plans; it is about motivating and leading staff to facilitate their work; and it is about monitoring and controlling all the processes in its responsibility.

To achieve all this, managers have to be able to communicate with their subordinates, bosses and peers effectively, to be able to look ahead and assess the future rationally and realistically, and they have to be able to guide and motivate those people around them to work well together towards stated objectives.

EFFECTIVE MANAGEMENT

A manager's effectiveness, or otherwise, can be judged not by what is done, but by what is achieved. Reddin (in *Managerial Effectiveness*, 1970) contrasts an effective manager with one who is merely efficient. An effective manager will do the right things, will produce new alternative solutions to problems, will optimize the utilization of the company's resources, will get new results, and will concentrate on increasing the company's profits. An efficient manager will merely do things the correct way, will solve problems as they occur, will safeguard the company's existing resources, will carry out set duties, and will concentrate upon lowering the company's costs. This is not bad management, far from it, but it is not truly effective management which helps the business to grow in strength and to expand.

It is the systematic making of profits by which management performance is ultimately judged.

Bibliography

Adair, J. (1974) *Management and Morality*. David & Charles.

Adair, J. (1985) *Effective Leadership: a self-development manual*. Gower.

Adair, J. (1986) *Effective Team Building*. Gower.

Adair, J. (1988) *Developing Leaders: the ten key principles*. Talbot.

Adams, J. S. (1963) Wage inequalities, productivity and quality. *Industrial Relations*,
vol. 3, pp. 261–275.

Argenti, J. (1980) *Practical Corporate Planning*. George Allen & Unwin.

Argyris, C. (1964) *Integrating the Individual and the Organization*. John Wiley.

Attwood, M. (1989) *Personnel Management*. Macmillan.

Blenkinsop, S. and Burns, N. (1992) Does your organisation get a clean bill of health? In *Journal of General Management*, vol. 18, no. 2, Winter, pp. 14–27.

Burns, T. and Stalker, G. (1971) *The Management of Innovation*. Tavistock Publications.

Campbell, J. P., Dunnette, M. D., Lawler, E. E. and Weick, K. (1970) *Managerial
Behavior, Performance and Effectiveness*. McGraw-Hill.

Carnall, C. and Maxwell, S. (1988) *Management: Principles and Policy*. ICSA Publishing.

Child, J. (1984) *Organization: A Guide to Problems and Practice*. Harper & Row.

Clarke, P. (1972) *Small Businesses – How They Survive and Succeed*. David & Charles.

Cole, G. A. (1986) *Personnel Management: Theory and Practice*. D. P. Publications.

Cyert, R. M. and March, J. G. (1963) *A Behavioural Theory of the Firm*. Prentice-Hall.

Deming, W. E. (1986) *Out of the Crisis, Quality, Productivity and Competitive Position*. Cambridge University Press.

Drucker, P. F. (1955) *The Practice of Management*. Heinemann.

Drucker, P. F. (1967) *A Theory of Leadership Effectiveness*. McGraw-Hill.

Eccles, R. G. (1991) The performance measurement manifesto. In *Harvard Business Review*, Jan–Feb, pp. 131–137.

Elbing, A. O. (1980) *Behavioural Decisions in Organizations* (2nd edn), Scott Foresman.

Emery, F. E. and Trist, E. L. (1965) The causal texture of organizational environments. *Human Relations*, February.

Fiedler, F. E. (1967) *A Theory of Leadership Effectiveness*. McGraw-Hill.

Gregory, A. J. and Jackson, G. (1989) The internal information systems function as a service operation. In *Systems Practice*, vol. X, no. X, pp. 37–39.

Handy, C. (1984) *Understanding Organizations*. Penguin.

Herzberg, F. (1966) *The Motivation to Work*.

Herzberg, F. (1966) *Work and the Nature of Man*. Staples Press.

Herzberg, F., Mausner, B. and Synderman, B. (1960) *The Motivation to Work*. John Wiley.

Howe, W. S. (1986) *Corporate Strategy*. Macmillan.

Humble, J. W. (1972) *Improving Business Results*. Pan Books.

Janis and Mann (1977) *Decision Making*. Free Press.

Jennings, E. E. (1977) *Routes to the Executive Suite*. McGraw-Hill.

Kaplan, R. S. and Norton, D. P. (1996) Using the balanced scorecard as a strategic management system. In *Harvard Business Review*, Jan–Feb, p. 75.

Kaplan, R. S. and Norton, D. P. (1992) The balanced scorecard – measures that drive performance. In *Harvard Business Review*, Jan–Feb, pp. 71–79.

Kast, F. E. and Rosenzweig, J. E. (1974) *Organization and Management: A Systems Approach*. McGraw-Hill.

Lawler, E. E. (1978) *Motivation and Work Organizations*. Brooks Cole Free Press.

Lawrence, P. R. and Lorsch, J. (1967) *Organization and Environment*. Richard D. Irwin.

Likert, R. (1967) *The Human Organization*. McGraw-Hill.

Luthaus, F. (1981) *Organizational Behaviour*. McGraw-Hill.

Lynch, R. L. and Cross, K. F. (1991) *Measure Up! Yardsticks for Continuous Improvement*. Blackwell Publishers.

McGregor, D. (1960) *The Human Side of Enterprise*. McGraw-Hill.

McClelland, D. C. (1967) *The Achieving Society*. Free Press.

McClelland, D. C. (1969) *Motivating Economic Achievement*. Free Press.

McClelland, D. C. (1972) *Motivation Workshops*. General Learning Press.

McClelland, D. C. (1985) *Human Motivation*. Scott Foresman.

March. J. G. and Simon, H. A. (1958) *Organization*. John Wiley.

Maslow, A. H. (1970) *Motivation and Personality*. Harper & Row.

Mintzberg, H. (1973) *The Nature of Managerial Work*. Harper & Row.

Pratt, K. (1988) Performance management. In *Management Services*, Dec, pp. 6–11.

Reddin, W. J. (1970) *Managerial Effectiveness*. McGraw-Hill.

Rees, W. D. (1984) *The Skills of Management*. Croom Helm.

Reicheld, F. F. and Sasser, W. (1990) 'Zero Defections: Quality comes to services. In *Harvard Business Review*, Sep–Oct, pp. 105–111.

Revans, R. W. (1971) *Developing Effective Managers: A New Approach to Business Education*. Longman.

Rockart, J. F. (1982) The changing role of the information systems executive: a critical success factor perspective. In *Sloan Management Review*, Fall.

Rodger, A. (1970) *The Seven Point Plan*. National Institute of Industrial Psychology.

Simon, H. A. (1959) *Administrative Behaviour*. Macmillan.

Stewart, R. (1977) *Managers and Their Jobs*. Macmillan.

Stewart, R. (1979) *The Reality of Management*. Pan Books.

Storey, D. J. (1982) *Entrepreneurship and the New Firm*. Croom Helm.

Tavsky, C. and Parke, E. L. (1976) Job enrichment, need theory and reinforcement theory. In R. Dublin (ed.) *Handbook of Work, Organizations and Society*. Rand McNally.

Taylor, F. (1911) *Principles of Scientific Management*.

Ullah, P. (1991) The psychology of TQM. *Managing Service Quality*, pp. 79–81.

Urwick, L. (1952) *Notes on the Theory of Organization*. American Management Association.

Urwick, L. (1958) *The Elements of Administration*. Pitman.

Vroom, V. H. (1964) *Work and Motivation*. John Wiley.

Woodward, J. (1965) *Industrial Organization: Theory and Practice*. Oxford University Press.

Yetton, P. W. and Vroom, V. H. (1978) The Vroom–Yetton model of leadership – an overview. In B. King, S. Strenfert and F. E. Fiedler (eds), *Managerial Control and Organizational Democracy*. John Wiley.

Zaire, M. (1992) *TQM based performance measurement practical guidelines*. Technical Communications (Publishing) Ltd.

Index